WOOD PATTERN-MAKING

WOOD PATTERN-MAKING

A TEXTBOOK

BY

HERBERT J. McCASLIN

Instructor in Pattern-making, Industrial Department, William L. Dickinson High School, Jersey City, N. J.

FIRST EDITION
THIRD IMPRESSION

McGRAW-HILL BOOK COMPANY, INC.
NEW YORK: 370 SEVENTH AVENUE
LONDON: 6 & 8 BOUVERIE ST., E. C. 4
1923

Wood Pattern Making

by Herbert J McCaslin

Originally published by
McGraw-Hill Book Company
New York
Original copyright 1923
by McGraw-Hill Book Company

Reprinted by
Lindsay Publications Inc
Bradley IL 60915

ISBN 1-55918-205-9

1997

4   5   6   7   8   9   10

WARNING

PREFACE

This book is for the student who desires to follow the occupation of pattern-making or who wishes to familiarize himself with the principles of the art. The text is based upon a series of problems which have been arranged in a progressive yet flexible manner, and which in the aggregate will constitute, (within a certain range) a course in pattern-making and a desirable preparation for more advanced work.

Problems have been selected or designed according to the principles of molding involved and to the difficulties encoun-tered in the construction of the pattern.

Very definite instructions are given pertaining to the order of operations required for the completion of these patterns. Repetition of instructions appearing in the text may seem unnecessary, but the experiences of twelve years as an instructor in pattern making have convinced the author that too much emphasis cannot be placed upon certain features.

It is not the intention of this book to deal with production methods as applied to patterns. The author is familiar with molding machine practices and their application to pro-duction work, and it is realized that if castings were desired in large numbers, many of the patterns required by the lessons would not be made as described.

The author's intention, however, is to follow those princi-ples of molding and pattern construction which have been established as good practice when a limited number of castings is required and the castings are to be made as individual molds.

The author wishes to acknowledge his appreciation and thanks to his fellow teachers, Carlos H. Handforth and Jay I. Henshaw, for their valuable aid. He also wishes to thank Frank E. Mathewson, Director of the Technical and Industrial

Department of the William L. Dickinson High School, for suggestions and advice incident to the publication of this book. Grateful acknowledgement is made to the American Wood Working Machinery Co., The Porter Cable Co. and The Oliver Machinery Co. for assistance.

HERBERT J. McCASLIN.

JERSEY CITY, N. J.
May, 1923.

TO THE STUDENT

Wood Pattern-making.—Objects made of cast metal are shaped by the process of founding. Founding, or foundry practice is that branch of the metal trades dealing with the melting of metals, and the pouring of these metals into molds that are usually made of sand.

It will, therefore, be seen that in order to shape the sand molds, some sort of *form* is required.

Making these forms, called *patterns*, is that branch of the metal trades known as pattern-making. It deals with the modeling of objects in wood, metal or other materials, that are intended to be cast in metal.

To become a successful pattern-maker, a thorough knowledge of the principles of *mechanical drawing and foundry practice* is necessary.

To many, this work may seem wholly a mechanical process, but it is, in fact, an art which requires a strong effort of the imagination, because all molding and construction features of a pattern must first be decided upon before actual work on the pattern is begun.

It may be said that no other metal trade affords a greater opportunity for the development of constructive ability than this work.

A sand mold is *destroyed* in the making of the casting, but any number of molds may be made by the use of a single pattern.

A model of an object cannot always be used as a pattern, because it may be of such form that it would be *impracticable to mold it.*

It is only in the production of small castings of certain form and requirements, that the pattern may be made an exact model of the object to be cast. Nearly all patterns require

vii

certain special features and allowances in their construction to *facilitate the molding,* as well as to produce a casting of *required form and dimensions.*

While the wood pattern-maker works in wood, the conditions that govern the construction of patterns in their accuracy and other requirements leave little in common between this artisan and those of other woodworking crafts.

The tools used in pattern-making do not differ from those used by other woodworkers except in the case of special tools that the particular needs of the trade have developed.

The method of procedure and the application of tools required by the instruction matter is not the only means whereby the pattern may be made. The application does, however, illustrate one of the means whereby the pattern may be completed.

The exercises are numbered one to eight inclusive. These exercises are to present certain principles and the application of the more common tools.

The special application of tools is a particular function of the individual lesson.

It is possible to follow the sequence as given, or to complete the exercise work by doing the turning lessons with the bench work.

Following the completion of the exercises, *Pattern* 1 must be completed in order that the *information regarding the requirements of a pattern may be obtained and applied to the lathe work.*

All concerns requiring objects cast in metal have some system of *numbering their patterns.* A common practice is to affix a raised number on the pattern so that it will appear in the casting. It is the means of keeping a record of the pattern, of *identifying* the casting and *checking up* the order list. To identify the pattern or part of pattern or core-box to follow; *each piece is to be stamped, or marked with the number of the pattern.*

MACHINES AND TOOLS

The pattern shop should include such machine tools as a combination saw-bench, a band-saw, a thickness planer, a jointer, a vertical boring machine with an assortment of Fostner bits, a trimmer, a disc and a spindle sander, an oil-grinder, a buffing-wheel, a band-saw filing machine. The lathe equipment should include a two jaw chuck for mounting work.

To help in the elimination of dust, all saws, planers, and sanding machines should be connected with a blower system.

In addition to the machine tools the shop equipment should include a medium size surface plate, and such bench tools as a core-box plane, a sole-plane, a draw knife, a surface gage, a large steel square, and large inside and outside calipers, and a set of $\frac{1}{8}$ inch and $\frac{1}{4}$ inch steel stencils (letters and figures).

In planning a pattern-maker's tool kit, the following list of tools will be found adequate for the ordinary run of work.

Awl—brad, $1\frac{1}{4}$ inch blade—flat point.
Bench brush.
Bevel—8 inches.
Bits—auger, $\frac{1}{4}$, $\frac{5}{16}$, $\frac{3}{8}$, $\frac{7}{16}$, $\frac{1}{2}$, and $\frac{9}{16}$ of an inch.
Bit—expansion, $\frac{5}{8}$ to $1\frac{3}{4}$ inches.
Bits—Fostner, $\frac{1}{2}$, $\frac{3}{4}$, and 1 inch.
Bits-twist, $\frac{3}{32}$, $\frac{1}{8}$, $\frac{5}{32}$, $\frac{3}{16}$, and $\frac{7}{32}$ of an inch.
Brace—ratchet, 8 inch sweep.
Calipers—outside, spring, 5 inch.
Calipers—inside, spring, 6 inch.
Calipers—outside, firm joint, 10 inch.
Chisels—paring, $\frac{1}{8}$, $\frac{1}{4}$, $\frac{1}{2}$, and 1 inch straight shank, long, beveled edge.
Chisels—paring $1\frac{1}{2}$ inch bent shank, long beveled edge.
Cornering tool, $\frac{1}{8}$ and $\frac{1}{4}$ inch.
Countersink.

Dividers—spring, 5 inch.

Dividers—8 inch, wing.

Fillet-irons, $\frac{1}{8}$, $\frac{1}{4}$, $\frac{3}{8}$, and $\frac{1}{2}$ inch.

Gouges—long bend, carving, $\frac{1}{4}$, $\frac{3}{8}$, and $\frac{1}{2}$ inch No. 18— $\frac{3}{4}$ inch No. 16—$\frac{7}{8}$ inch No. 14.

Gouges—short bend, carving, $\frac{1}{4}$, $\frac{3}{8}$, $\frac{5}{8}$, and 1 inch No. 18.

Gouges—paring, $\frac{1}{8}$ and $\frac{1}{4}$ inch straight shank, regular sweep.

Gouges—paring $\frac{3}{8}$, $\frac{1}{2}$, and $\frac{5}{8}$ inch bent shank, regular sweep.

Gouges—paring, $\frac{3}{4}$, 1, $1\frac{1}{4}$ inch bent shank, middle sweep.

Gouges—paring, $\frac{1}{2}$, $\frac{3}{4}$, and $1\frac{1}{4}$ inch bent shank, flat sweep.

Hammer—carpenter, 13 ounces.

Hand-drill.

Knife-bench.

Leather-strop.

Marking-gage.

Nail-sets, $\frac{1}{32}$, and $\frac{1}{16}$ inch, cupped point.

Oil-stone—India, 2 $\times$ 8 inches.

Oil-stone—slip-stone $1\frac{3}{4}$ $\times$ $4\frac{1}{2}$ inches, $\frac{1}{8}$ and $\frac{3}{8}$ Radii.

Pinchers—carpenter, 6 inch.

Pinch dogs, 1 and $1\frac{1}{2}$ inch.

Plane—fore, 18 inches.

Plane—smooth, 8 inches.

Plane—rabbet, $\frac{3}{4}$ inch.

Plane—router

Rule—contraction, $\frac{1}{10}$ of an inch per foot.

Rule—contraction, $\frac{5}{32}$ of an inch per foot.

Rule—contraction, $\frac{2}{10}$ of an inch per foot.

Rule—standard.

Saw—cross-cut, 20 inch, 8 point.

Saw—compass.

Square—combination, center-head and protractor.

Screw-driver—bits, $\frac{1}{4}$ and $\frac{3}{8}$ of an inch width of tip.

Screw-driver—$\frac{3}{16}$ of an inch in diameter, $4\frac{1}{2}$ inch blade.

Screw-driver—$\frac{5}{16}$ of an inch in diameter, 6 inch blade.

Spoke-shaves—1½ and 2½ inch blades.
Trammels.

TURNING TOOLS

Turning tools.
Diamond-point, ¾ inch.
Gouge—1 inch.
Flat chisels—½ and 1 inch.
Parting-tool— ⅝ inch.
Round-nose tools—⅜ and ¾ inch.
Side-tools —⅜ inch, right and left-hand.
Skew-chisel—¾ inch.

The usefulness of tools depends upon the condition in which they are kept.

CONTENTS

PART I
BENCH WORK

PART II
LATHE WORK

PART I
BENCH WORK

WOOD PATTERN-MAKING

PATTERN WOODS

Pattern Woods.—Wood possesses certain qualities necessary in the construction of large and small patterns at moderate cost, that are found to the same degree in no other material. Woods are selected that have a *comparatively straight, close grain, that may be easily cut and that have little tendency to change shape when exposed to moisture.* The best lumber is

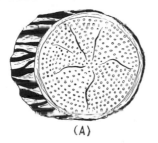
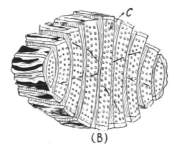
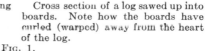

<table>
<tr><td align="center">(A)</td><td align="center">(B)</td></tr>
</table>

Cross section of a log illustrating the growth rings.

Cross section of a log sawed up into boards. Note how the boards have curled (warped) away from the heart of the log.

FIG. 1.

always cut from mature trees, the fibers of which have become compact through the drying of the sap and from the external pressure exerted by the bark.

If the cross section of a log as shown in Fig. 1, A, be closely examined, it will be observed to be made up of concentric rings extending from the center of the log to the outside. The rings are composed of numerous little *tubes or cells* through which the sap is conveyed throughout the tree. The rings are called *year- or growth-rings*, and as one ring is usually

1

added each year the tree continues to grow, the approximate age of the tree can be reckoned by counting the rings.

The varying amount of moisture in wood changes the diameter of the little tubes or cells, thus causing the board to *shrink or swell*. As the tubes are in the direction of the board's length, little or no *lengthwise change takes place*. When a log is sawn up into boards, as shown in Fig. 1, B, the tendency of the boards is to curl away (*warp*), as shown, from the side which was toward the heart or the center of the log. This is due to a greater amount of *shrinkage* taking place in the wood tissue toward the outside of the tree. Observation shows that a board cut from the center of a log, as at *C* and having an *equal distribution of the growth rings*, is likely to remain straight.

The straightness of grain in a board is determined by the appearance of the sawn face, which should present a uniform roughness over its entire surface. Boards with a *twisted or fancy grain should always be avoided*. The expression *"wind"* as applied to a board means that the board is *twisted*. Wind in a board may be caused by a board not lying flat while drying out, or it may be caused by an uneven strain due to a crooked or fancy grain.

The presence of an unusual amount of *pitch* in a board is betrayed by its weight, which will be excessive. Such a board will prove hard to work, and will not make a *dependable pattern*. Only *dry lumber* should be used for pattern work. A dry board will feel dry to the hands and, if free from pitch, will be reasonably light.

If a well-seasoned board, planed straight and true, be laid upon a flat surface for any length of time, the tendency of the upper surface will be to curl up or warp. This is due to the upper or exposed side *drying* out more freely than the under side, which is protected from the air. For this reason, after planing stock to thickness, it should always be placed so that the *air may circulate freely about it*.

Kiln-dried and Air-dried Lumber.—Kiln-dried lumber is lumber in which the seasoning or drying process is hastened by placing the boards in a drying room or kiln. *Seasoned or air-dried* lumber is lumber that is permitted to dry naturally under sheds. It is so piled as to allow a free circulation of air. Seasoned lumber is superior to kiln-dried, as the rapid drying destroys much of the natural elasticity of the wood fibers, making them brittle and harder to work.

Of the woods chiefly employed for pattern purposes, *white pine* continues to furnish the principal supply. Throughout the Western States, *redwood* has been largely used in this work. For patterns which are subjected to rough usage or used in making many castings, harder woods such as *mahogany*, *cherry* or *maple* are often selected.

Measuring Lumber.—A board foot measures 12 inches by 12 inches by 1 inch. To compute the number of feet in a board, multiply the length in *feet* by the width in *inches* by the thickness in *inches* and divide the product by 12.

Lumber is usually sold at a certain price per hundred feet or per thousand feet. The letter C is commonly used to indicate one hundred feet and the letter M one thousand feet.

QUESTIONS

1. What qualities should wood for pattern work possess?
2. From what kind of trees is the best lumber cut?
3. What is understood by year- or growth-rings?
4. How is the sap conveyed throughout a tree?
5. How may the age of a tree be closely reckoned?
6. What causes a board to shrink or swell?
7. Why does moisture not affect a board in the direction of its length?
8. Why will the surface of a board which was toward the heart of the tree become convexed?
9. Why will a board cut from the center of a log be more apt to remain straight?
10. How may the straightness of grain in a board be determined?
11. How is the presence of an unusual amount of pitch in a board betrayed?
12. Why should a board containing an unusual amount of pitch be avoided?
13. Why should only dry lumber be used for pattern work?
14. What test may be given a board for dryness?

The Plane.—The *bench-plane*, as illustrated in Fig. 2, is the type chiefly used by the pattern-maker to reduce or smooth the surface of a board. Planes vary in length from 7 inches to 30 inches. Those under 14 inches in length are termed *smoothing-planes*. They are used to produce a smooth but not a true surface.

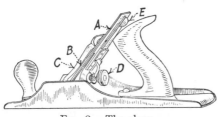

FIG. 2.—The plane.

Jack-plane is the name given the planes of 14- and 15-inch length. It is the plane used for general work.

Jointer is the name given the planes exceeding 15 inches in length. The 18- and 20-inch length planes are often termed *fore-planes.* They are used to plane large surfaces and the edges of boards so that they can be closely fitted together. The *longer the plane,* the more accurate will be the surface produced.

Since the length of the rough stock from which the exercises and patterns to follow are to be made does not exceed 16 inches, the *jack-plane* will be used.

There are two chief adjustments in the plane illustrated. When the *bit A* is secured in the plane with the *clamp C,* the use of the *thumb-screw D* will move the bit up or down and thus the thickness of the shaving to be taken from the material can be regulated. By the use of the *lever E,* located under the bit, and working sidewise, the cutting edge of the bit is brought into position with the sole or face of the plane. The *bit A and cap B* are secured together with a screw. The function of the *cap B* is to stiffen the bit and to prevent chattering.

The splitting of the wood in advance of the cutting edge of the bit is prevented by the curling up and breaking of the shaving as it hits against the cap. The cap is set back about $\frac{1}{32}$ of an inch from the cutting edge of the bit.

Form the habit of sighting along the sole before beginning to plane, in order to see that the adjustment of the bit is correct.

The beginner must first learn how a tool must be sharpened; he must then acquire, by practice, the knack of doing it.

Grinding a Plane-bit.—When the repeated whetting of a plane-bit has increased the angle, or rounded the ground surface of the bit to the extent that it does not *cut easily or smoothly*, it should be *ground*. The included angle of the cutting edge should be ground to approximately 22 *degrees*. Figure 3 illustrates a plane-bit being ground. The bit is moved back and forth across the face of the stone.

The Oil-grinder.—The oil-grinder has succeeded the large grind-stone in the modern pattern shop. Figure 3 illustrates a plane-bit held in a fixture at *A*. A groove in the platform e n g a g e s the holder. The holder is caused to move back and forth in front of the stone.

When grinding a plane-bit or any edge tool, particular care must be taken *not to bear on too hard*, or the edge of the tool will become *over heated and the temper lost*.

Fɪɢ. 3.—A plane-bit held in a fixture while being ground.

Edge tools are ground with the stone *revolving* towards the tool.

Whetting.—Following the grinding, the plane bit is *whetted* upon an oil-stone to a keen cutting edge. The ground surface of the bit is placed upon the stone, as shown in Fig. 4. While steadily held in this position, the bit is rubbed over the face of the stone, *along an elliptical path*. Passing the bit over the surface of the stone along an elliptical path produces a straight cutting edge and causes the surface of the stone to be worn down more evenly.

For the beginner, the plane will be found a little more easy to operate if the cutting edge of the bit is given an amount of *crown*—(rounded to the extent of a thin shaving). Crown is given the edge when whetting it, by exerting a little more pressure toward the ends of the edge.

As one becomes more experienced, the cutting edge should be kept straight and the corners slightly rounded. *To avoid unnecessary grinding, the bit should be held against the oil-stone as near at the angle to which it was ground as possible.*

If the cutting edge on the face of the blade is examined after this operation, a slight roughness, or what is called a *wire-edge,* will be found. The wire-edge is removed by holding the face of the bit flat upon the stone as shown in Fig. 5, then rubbing it back and forth in the direction of the stone's length.

   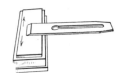

FIG. 4.—Whetting the ground surface of   FIG. 5.—Whetting the face of
        a plane-bit.   a plane-bit.

By reversing the operation of whetting first the ground surface of the bit, then the face of the bit, the wire-edge is removed. That the flatness of the face of the bit may not be impaired, always hold the face of the bit *firmly down* upon the stone.

Free use of oil washes off the small particles of metal cut from the tool and prevents the glazing of the surface of the stone.

Testing the Edge.—The sharpness of the edge may be tested by lightly drawing the tip of the thumb along it. If it feels *rough or jagged,* it has not been properly whetted. If the edge has been properly whetted, it will score the skin deeply enough to be felt, and it will be realized that a slight pressure will cause it to cut through. The edge of a bit made dull through usage will feel smooth, and it *should be whetted.*

Stropping.—Following the whetting of a plane bit, the edge is *stropped* by being drawn over the surface of a strip of leather affixed to a block. In stropping the edge, always hold the bit so as to keep the ground surface of the bit as *near at the angle* to which it was ground as possible, and the face of the bit *flat* upon the surface of the leather.

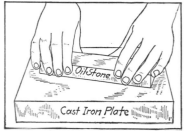

FIG. 6.—Truing up the surface of an oil-stone.

Truing Up the Surface of an Oil-stone.—When the surface of an oil-stone shows indications of wear or becomes uneven, it should be *trued up*. This is done by moistening the finished surface of a cast iron plate with gasoline, then sprinkling over it a small amount of medium grade emery. The surface of the stone is then applied to the surface of the plate as shown in Fig. 6. The stone is rubbed over the surface of the plate along a circular path.

FIG. 7.—Motor driven jointer.

The Jointer.—The jointer as illustrated in Fig. 7 is a planing machine. The various planing operations to which it lends itself makes it one of the most useful adjuncts to a pattern-shop equipment. The size of a jointer is specified by the length of the head or knives in inches and is known as an 8 inch or a 12 inch, accordingly.

There is always more or less of an element of *danger* connected with the operation of all power-driven wood-working machines; *therefore, a beginner should never attempt to use a power-driven machine until its control and use have been thoroughly explained and demonstrated by a competent operator.*

QUESTIONS

1. What causes a board to curl up when laid upon a flat surface?

2. What precaution may be taken to keep a board from warping?

3. What is kiln-dried lumber?

4. What is seasoned or air-dried lumber?

5. Why is seasoned or air-dried lumber superior to kiln-dried lumber?

6. What woods are chiefly used for pattern work?

7. What is the number of board feet in a board 8½ feet long, 9 inches wide and 1½ inches thick?

8. For what work is a smoothing-plane chiefly used?

9. For what work is a jack-plane chiefly used?

10. For what work is a jointer chiefly used?

11. What is the object of the cap which is attached to a plane-bit?

12. About how far back should the cap be set from the cutting-edge of the bit?

13. What are the indications that a bit is in need of grinding?

14. To about what angle should a plane-bit be ground?

15. What is apt to occur if too much pressure is exerted upon a tool while being ground?

16. When whetting a bit, what is the object in causing it to follow an elliptical path?

17. What does the term crown mean as applied to the cutting-edge of a bit?

18. When whetting a plane-bit, why should it be held against the stone as near to the angle to which it was ground as possible?

19. What is understood by the term wire-edge?

20. How is a wire-edge removed?

21. How may the sharpness of the cutting-edge of a plane-bit be tested?

22. How may the surface of an oil-stone be trued up?

23. In what direction should the grinding wheel revolve with respect to the tool being ground?

24. Why should plenty of oil be used on an oil-stone?

EXERCISE 1

Features presented:
Planing
Testing with a try-square surfaces which are at right
    angles
Gaging of lines
Laying off distances
Scribing lines with a knife
Band-sawing

Figure 8 is the drawing of Exercise 1.

When beginning work on an exercise or pattern, it should
be definitely understood *what* is to be made, *how* it is to be

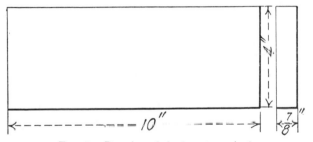

FIG. 8. Drawing of the board required.

made, and *why* it is to be made in the *manner chosen.* *For
this reason* the student should carefully read all of the instructions before beginning work upon an exercise.

Pencil lines, while accurate enough for many purposes,
are inexact when *defining* close dimensions. A scratch or
a dent cannot be called *a line*, and carelessness in this direction will be manifested in the finished work.

No feature in pattern construction requires greater care
than the correct establishing of *true surfaces or lines* from which

9

dimensions are to begin. No work is more important than that relating to the location and *production* of these surfaces and lines. Lines drawn in the direction of the grain of the wood are to be *scribed with the gage*. Lines which lie across the grain of the wood are to *be scribed with the knife*. Knife lines must be deep and clean cut. The expression, *"work to the line," means splitting the line.*

Planing a piece of work to given dimensions is a reducing process. In order to accomplish this end, the rough stock is

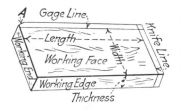

FIG. 9.—The length and width dimensions of the board laid off upon the material.

sawed larger than the size of the object when completed. The amount of waste material to be removed will depend somewhat upon the size and shape of the object. For the ordinary run of small objects, ⅛ *inch* in thickness, ¼ *inch* in width, and ½ *inch* in length, will be found sufficient.

The exercise to be made is a rectangular board of a given thickness, width and length. Figure 9 shows the work in process of making; the wood has been planed to the required thickness, the working end planed, and the width and length scribed upon each face.

The stock required is 1 inch thick, 4¼ inches wide, and 10½ inches long, or, *as usually written*, 1 × 4¼ × 10½ inches.

ORDER OF OPERATIONS

1. Plane true one face of the material; for reference, call and mark it the *working face*.

If there be any *warp or wind* in the surface of a board to be planed, this should be determined first of all. This is done by tilting the plane on its long corner edge while the worker looks between the board and the plane, toward the light. The plane must be placed in various directions across the board. If the distance between the diagonal corners of the board exceeds the length of the plane, then the straight edge of a strip must be used for testing the surface.

In planing a surface of a board that is in wind, *the high corners are noted and planed down first.* The first plane stroke should be along the edge, either beginning or ending at a point near the center of the length of the board. The next stroke should be somewhat shorter, and they should continue to decrease as the planing proceeds toward the middle of the width of the board. To terminate a cut at about a certain point in the board's length, the toe of the plane is lifted. When the wind has been removed, proceed to plane the entire surface.

The Bench-stop.—The bench-stop as indicated by *A*, Fig. 10, is the most efficient way of holding material to be planed, flat upon the bench. If the direction of the cut is kept parallel with the long edges of the surface being planed, the material will not shift its position.

FIG. 10.—Planing the face of the board.

Place the end of the board as shown against the *bench-stop* and take a position well back, so that the plane may be pushed to arm's length.

Do not make the mistake of trying to take a heavy cut.

Should the grain of wood *tear out*, and the surface become *rough*, turn the board around so as to begin the stroke from the opposite end of the board, and with the grain of the wood. *Note the effect on the planed surface.*

As about two thirds of the plane's length overhangs the end of the board when starting the stroke, the forward end of the plane should be held down firmly, by pressure exerted upon the knob, until the plane is well on the board, at which time the pressure should be the same on both knob and handle. As the forward end of the plane passes off the board, the pressure should be exerted upon the handle.

A *true surface* cannot be produced unless the sole of the plane lies flat upon the board throughout the length of the cut.

As the planing proceeds, the trueness of the surface should be tested from time to time with the long corner edge of the plane.

2. Plane straight and square with the *working face* one of the edges of the material; call and mark it the *working edge.*

An edge surface of a board is more easily planed if the board is held in a vise.

The Try-square.—The accuracy of the *working edge* in its relation to the *working face* is tested with a *try-square as shown*

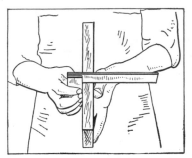

in Fig. 11. Hold the square loosely in the right hand, grasping the stock as shown. Press the edge of the stock firmly against the working face, allowing the edge of the blade to touch lightly the surface of the working edge. The edge should be *tested* throughout its length.

Fig. 11.—Testing the edge of the board with a try square.

From one of these two dressed surfaces, *working face and working edge,* all other dimensions of the board are to be gaged or squared preparatory to reducing the material to size.

3. Set the *marking-gage* to the required thickness of board, then from the *working face,* gage lines upon the *ends and edges.*

Marking-gage.—The marking-gage, is used for *gaging lines* parallel to a corner edge of a board. It consists of a bar which carries a sliding head. The head is secured at any point in the bar's length by a thumb-nut. The spur that does the scribing is inserted through the bar near one end. The gage is set to the approximate distance, then the final adjustment made by lightly tapping the end of the bar on the bench to move it in or out.

A dimension is taken from a rule with a marking-gage as shown in Fig. 12, A. The marking-gage is used as shown in Fig. 12, B. The depth of a gage line is regulated by tilting or rolling the gage from you. The *spur* should be kept sharp so that it will produce a *clean-cut line.* The head of the gage must always be kept *firmly pressed* against the surface from which the lines are being gaged. Failure to so hold the gage will result in the spur leaving its *desired course.*

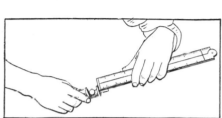

Fig. 12, A.—Taking a dimension from a rule with a marking-gage.

Fig. 12, B.—Gaging upon the edges of the board the required thickness.

4. Plane the material to thickness, *split the line.*

5. From the *working edge*, gage the required width of board upon each face.

Caution: Do not dress the board to width.

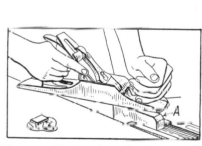

Fig. 13.—Planing the end surface of the board.

Fig. 14.—Testing the end surface of the board with a try square.

6. Plane straight and square to working face and working edge one of the ends of the material; call and mark it the *working end.*

The board is held in the vise as illustrated in Fig. 13. Hold the plane at an angle as shown, in order that the fiber of the grain of wood shall be severed by a shearing cut. *Note* how the corner indicated by *A is chamfered* to prevent the splitting out of the grain of wood while planing the end surface.

The plane is held at an angle, but the direction of the stroke is parallel with the long edge corners of the surface being planed. The *squareness* of the corner formed by the working edge and the working end is *tested* with the square, as shown in Fig. 14.

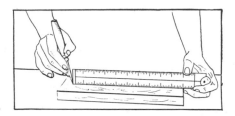

Fig. 15.—Laying off from the working end, the length dimension of the board.

7. Lay off from the working end the required length of the board, and scribe a *knife-line* around the material.

The length dimension of the board is laid off by placing the rule upon its edge as shown in Fig. 15. While the 10-inch graduation mark is made to exactly coincide with the edge cor-

Fig. 16.—Squaring a line across the face of the board.

ner of the working end, the point of the knife is placed at the end of the rule as shown.

The try-square with the stock bearing against the working edge is now slid along until the blade of the square touches the blade of the knife as shown in Fig. 16. Hold the stock of the square *firmly against the working edge,* and draw the knife along, pressing it lightly against the blade of the square. To prevent the knife from running away from the blade of the square, turn the edge of the knife slightly toward the blade.

8. About $\frac{1}{32}$ inch outside or on the waste side of this line, saw off the waste material; then plane the *end* surface down to the line.

Attention is again called to the *chamfered corner* as at *A,* Fig. 13.

9. About $\frac{1}{32}$ inch on the waste side of the line representing the *width* of the board, Fig. 9, saw off the waste material; then plane this edge surface down to the line.

Fig. 17.—The band-saw.

The Band-saw.—The band-saw as illustrated in Fig. 17 is used for all kinds of curved and combinations of straight and curved sawing. The table may be tilted 45 degrees to the right and 30 degrees to the left.

The size of a band-saw is specified by the diameter in inches of the wheels over which the saw runs.

QUESTIONS

1. What should be definitely understood before beginning work on an exercise or pattern?

2. What is the advantage of lines scribed with a knife over those drawn with a pencil?

3. What tool is used to scribe lines which lie in the direction of the grain of the wood?

4. Why is a knife used to scribe lines which lie across the grain of the wood?

5. What does the term splitting a line mean?

6. What is understood by the term working face?   working edge? working end?

7. Why is the accuracy of these surfaces very important?

8. What is understood by the term warp or wind, as applied to a board?

9. How is a board tested to determine if it is warped?

10. How is a board tested for wind?

11. What is the procedure in reducing with the plane a surface that is in wind?

12. What is a bench-stop?

13. How should the pressure be distributed upon a plane from the beginning to the completion of a cut?

14. How is the accuracy of the working edge in its relation to the working face tested?

15. Describe and give the names of the different parts of the marking-gage.

16. How is the final or close adjustment of a gage made?

17. Why should the head of the gage always be held firmly against the surface from which the line is being gaged?

18. What is the object in holding a plane at an angle to the face of a board when planing end grain wood?

19. What may be done to prevent the splitting out of the wood while planing the end of a board?

20. How should the rule be placed upon a surface when laying off or measuring a dimension?

21. Name in order the operations required in planing a board to a given thickness, width and length.

EXERCISE 2

Features presented:
Laying out an irregular object.
Planing across the grain of wood at an angle other than
90 degrees.
Figure 18 is the drawing of Exercise **2.**
Careful workmanship is the foremost requirement in pattern-
making, and should be *developed* from the very start. The
exercise to be made is a board of an irregular outline.

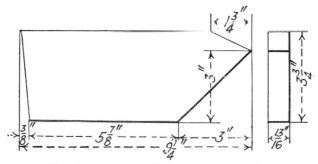

Fig. 18.—Drawing of the object to be made.

The ends of the object are not square with the edges, but
form angles other than 90 degrees. This exercise not only
assists in the development of accuracy in laying out work, but
affords practice in planing surfaces which are other than 90
degrees to that of the grain of wood.

This exercise in process of making is shown in Fig. 19. The
wood has been planed to the required thickness, the working
edge prepared, and the shape of the object laid out upon each
face of the material, preparatory to sawing and planing it to
shape. For the purpose of reference, letters are used to designate the given dimensions of the object.

2   17

The arrow heads indicate the direction of the cut when planing surfaces which lie at an angle other than 90 degrees to the grain of wood.   The grain of wood will have a tendency to be raised by the plane-bit and *torn out* instead of *severed*, if the cut is made in the opposite direction.   This is due to the fibrous structure of the wood.

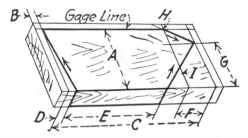

Fig. 19.—The shape of the object laid out upon the material.

Particular attention is called to the fact that the layout on both sides of the material is to be made *following the sequence of steps as listed.*   If the layout is made on one side and then on the other, an unnecessary handling of tools will result. *Following the steps as listed promotes accuracy and eliminates loss of time.*

At the completion of a layout, carefully check or *verify* all dimensions of the object with those on the *drawing.*

The stock required is: 1 × 4 × 10 inches, or the object may be made from the preceding exercise.

ORDER OF OPERATIONS

1. As in the preceding exercise, plane the material to the *required thickness* of the object, and make a *working edge.*

Note.—For the bench exercises and patterns to follow, this operation will be known as: *Prepare the material.*

2. Begin the layout by gaging upon each face the width dimension as represented by the letter *A* in Fig. 19.

3. Determine how much longer the material is than the object; lay off one half of this amount from one end as represented by the letter B, and scribe a line about the material.

4. From this line lay off the over-all length of the object as shown by the letter C, and scribe this line about the material.

5. Lay off and scribe lines across the working edge, which represent the dimensions D, E, and F.

6. Dimension F locates the line I; scribe this line across each face until it intersects the gage line at H.

7. From the working edge gage the distance G, then complete the layout by connecting the points thus located with *well defined knife lines*. Use the blade of the square as a straight edge when scribing these lines.

8. About $\frac{1}{32}$ inch outside of the lines which represent the angular ends, saw off the waste material.

0. Plane the end surfaces down to the center of the knife lines.

10. Saw and plane the object to the required width.

EXERCISE 3

Features presented:
Application of center lines.
Taking a dimension from a rule with the dividers.
Chisel paring.
Figure 20 is the drawing of Exercise **3.**
No other feature in pattern work *assures* greater accuracy than that of *true center lines.* Their purpose is to serve as

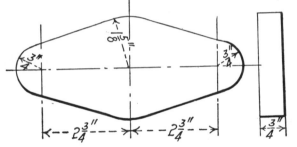

Fig. 20.—Drawing of the object to be made.

a *basis or starting point* from which dimensions are to be measured.

This exercise presents the use of *center lines.* It will show the *error* that will result if they are not accurately scribed or placed in their proper relation to one another.

If the intersection of center lines *A, B* and *D* Fig. 21 do not locate on one face, directly opposite the intersection point on the reverse face of the material, the edge surface of the object will not be *true to form.*

The operation of checking or verifying the dimensions of a pattern with those on the drawing, requires that all *center lines appear upon the finished work.*

20

Figure 21 shows how the shape of the object is to appear upon both faces of the material, when it is ready to be sawed to within about ⅟₃₂ inch of its scribed outline.

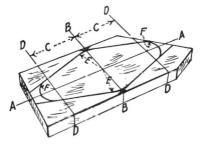

FIG. 21.—The shape of the object laid out upon the material.

The stock required is ⅞ × 3¾ × 7½ inches, or the object made from the preceding exercise as shown in Fig. 21.

ORDER OF OPERATIONS

1. Prepare the material.
2. Gage *center line A* upon each face along the middle of its width.
3. At the middle of the length of center line *A*, locate and scribe about the material *the center line B*.
4. From the intersection of center lines *A* and *B*, lay off upon *A* the dimensions represented by *C*. *Use the dividers.*

Dividers.—Dividers are used for measuring distances between points, for transferring distances taken from a rule, for scribing arcs and circles, and for the subdividing of lines. Figure 22 shows how a dimension is taken from a rule with dividers of the wing type.

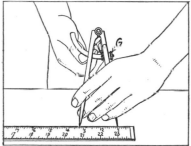

FIG. 22.—Taking a dimension from a rule with dividers.

Wing dividers are provided with an adjusting nut as indicated by *G*, which is very useful in adding to or subtracting from, the original setting.

In using dividers, grasp them in the right hand at the top where the two legs are joined together. When scribing a circle, rotate the dividers from left to right around to the starting point. Go over the surface very *lightly*, for any attempt to scribe a deep line will probably cause the point to follow the grain of wood, thus causing the line to be irregular.

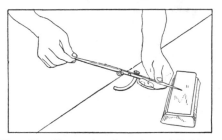

Fig. 23.—Sharpening the points of dividers.

Whenever *distances* are the *same* about a given point or each side of a center line, as the dimension represented by *C*, the *dividers* are used to lay off these distances.

The points should always be kept sharp. This is done by holding the point on an oil-stone as shown in Fig. 23, and, while passing it back and forth in the direction of the stone's length, rotating it one way and then the other.

5. Scribe about the material the *center lines D*.

6. Set the dividers to the dimension represented by *E*, and with the intersection of *lines A and B as the center*, scribe arcs as shown.

7. Set the dividers to the dimension represented by *F*, and with the intersection of *lines A and D as the center*, scribe arcs as shown.

8. Scribe lines tangent to the arcs.

9. Saw within $\frac{1}{32}$ inch *of the scribed outline*.

10. Plane to the center of the lines that are scribed tangent to the arcs. Pare to the center of lines of the scribed arcs.

The Paring-chisel.—A long thin chisel with either square or beveled edges. Chisels of $1\frac{1}{4}$ or $1\frac{1}{2}$ inches in width are chiefly used for paring. Grasp the chisel in the *right hand*, well down on the blade as shown in Fig. 24. Hold the material firmly with the left hand, at the same time guiding the chisel along the line with the thumb. As pressure is exerted upon the chisel, it is drawn to the right or left, producing a slicing cut.

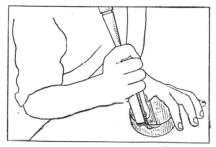

FIG. 24.—Position of holding a paring-chisel.

Tilt the handle slightly to *avoid* under-cutting the surface. *Pare from one face and then from the other*, until a true surface is produced. As the paring proceeds, the surface should be tested with the long corner edge of the chisel.

A chisel is ground and whetted in the same manner as a plane-bit.

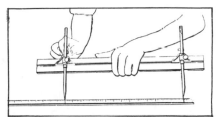

FIG. 25.—Taking a dimension from a rule with the trammels.

Trammels.—A wooden bar supporting two sliding heads that carry steel points used for distances and dimensions that exceed the limit of the dividers.

Figure 25 illustrates how the trammels are held while taking a dimension from rule.

EXERCISE 4

Features presented:

    Scribing an arc, the center of which lies outside the limit of the material

    Gouge-paring

    Grinding a paring-gouge

    Whetting a paring-gouge

    Stropping and buffing the edge of a gouge

Figure 26 is the drawing of Exercise **4.** This exercise consists of a rectangular figure containing a concave surface in each edge.

Figure 27 shows the shape of the object as it is to appear upon each face of the material when ready to shape the concave surfaces.

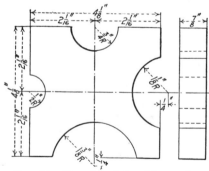

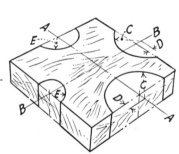

FIG. 26.—Drawing of the object to be made.   FIG. 27.—The shape of the object laid out upon the material.

Frequently the center of an arc will fall upon the *edge or outside the limit* of the material, as in the case of the radii *C*. To locate such centers, square up two edges of a block, then square a line across one of the surfaces. Upon this line gage the distance represented by *D*.

24

To scribe the arc, locate and firmly hold the block against the edge of the work as shown in Fig. 28. Except for the purpose of illustration there is no particular reason why the spring dividers, as shown, be used in preference to the wing dividers. When the center occurs upon the edge of the material, as in the case of radii *E*, it is only necessary to hold a block against this surface.

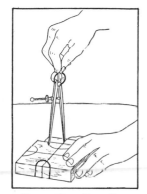

When the layout of an object has been completed, the scribed or gaged lines may be further *defined* with a medium-hard chisel-pointed pencil.

The Paring-gouge.—When *straight or convexed* surfaces are to be reduced by paring, the *chisel* is used. When *concave* surfaces are to be pared, the *paring-gouge* is used. It is often termed an inside ground gouge. A

Fig. 28 — Locating a point of the dividers outside of the limit of the material.

paring-gouge has the angle of the cutting edge ground on the *inside* or concave face of the blade.

The object in the previous exercise had an irregular outline. There is no advantage in dressing the material for an object of an irregular outline to the over-all length and width dimensions, then sawing it to shape.

The general outline of Exercise **4,** being of regular form, the material is more easily planed to the length and width dimensions before the concave surfaces are dressed to shape.

The stock required is 1 × 4⅜ × 4½ inches.

ORDER OF OPERATIONS

1. Prepare the material.
2. Dress to length, then to width.
3. Scribe the center line *A* at the middle of its length, and gage the center line *B* along the middle of its width.

4. Scribe the outline of the concave surfaces, then establish their width upon the edges by scribing knife lines across the edges, as shown.

5. Remove the excess waste material of openings with *band-saw.* One thirty-second inch is to be allowed upon the wall of the openings for paring the surface to the required outline.

If a saw-blade of ¼ inch width were used, it would be possible to saw to the line of the scribed arcs made with a 1⅛- and 1⅜-inch radius. For the beginner, it will be safer to make a series of *straight cuts,* $\frac{1}{16}$ inch apart, at right angles to the edge of the material and within $\frac{1}{32}$ inch of the line, then break out the material between the saw cuts.

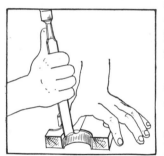

FIG. 29.—Position of holding a paring-gouge.

6. Select a gouge of the *same or of a slightly less radius than the surface to be pared.*

7. The gouge is grasped well down on the blade by the right hand as shown in, Fig. 29.

While pressure exerted by the thumb of the left hand holds the work, it at the same time controls the placing of the cutting edge of the gouge. As pressure is placed upon the gouge, it is slightly *oscillated,* and thereby caused to *sever* the grain of wood more easily and smoothly. *Tilt* the handle of the gouge slightly, to prevent under-cutting.

Pare from one face of the material and then from the other, until a *true surface is produced.* As the paring proceeds, the surface should be tested with the long corner edge of the gouge.

Grinding.—A narrow convexed face abrasive wheel is best suited for this work. Keep the gouge *rocking* one way and then the other, that the surface ground will be continuous and the thickness of the cutting edge *uniform.*

Hold the gouge *lightly,* that it may be guided by a *sensitive touch.*

The contact between the gouge and the stone must be of *short duration* and the edge of the gouge *cooled* by submerging it in water between applications.

Whetting.—Figure 30 illustrates how a paring-gouge is whetted. Hold the slip-stone at the proper angle to the face of the blade. Give the slip-stone a *lengthwise movement*, at the same time moving it back and forth along the entire length of the cutting edge.

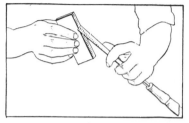

Slip or Slip-stone.—The type used by the pattern-maker is of a diminishing thickness, h a v i n g edges

FIG. 30.—Whetting the concave face of a paring-gouge with a slip-stone.

straight longitudinally but curved in section for the adaptation to the concave surface of gouges.

Hold the *convexed* face of the blade firmly down upon an *oil-stone*, and give it a *rocking motion* while moving it back and forth in the direction of the stone's length.

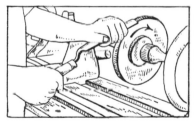

FIG. 31.—Buffing the edge of a paring-gouge.

To further sharpen the edge, it is stropped by being drawn, first the concave, then the convex face, over a piece of leather.

The Buffing-wheel. — Figure 31 illustrates a buffing-wheel made up of many thicknesses of cotton cloth sewed together. When used with *good judgment* and a very fine grade of polishing material, it becomes a very useful device in stropping gouges. *A buffing-wheel revolves from the tool.*

The paring-gouge illustrated has a bent shank. This type of gouge is especially adapted to the dressing of long concave surfaces.

QUESTIONS

1. In what direction should the cut be made when planing end grain wood, the surface of which forms an angle other than 90 degrees with the direction of the grain?

2. What is understood by the expression, "Check the layout of the work."

3. What is a straight-edge?

4. What is the object of center lines?

5. For what purposes are dividers used?

6. What should be avoided when scribing an arc or a circle upon the surface of wood?

7. What is understood by tangent?

8. What is understood by the expression chisel-paring?

9. How is a slicing cut produced with a chisel?

10. What is the difference between a chisel and a gouge?

11. Is the angle of the cutting-edge of a paring-gouge ground on the convex or concave face of the blade?

12. Why is a gouge slightly oscillated about its axis when used for paring?

13. How is the angle of the cutting-edge of a paring-gouge best ground?

14. What is liable to happen if too much pressure is placed upon a tool when grinding it?

15. What is understood by the term whetting?

16. What is understood by the term stropping?

17. How is the selection of a paring-gouge made in regards to the surface to be dressed?

18. How and of what material is a buffing-wheel made?

EXERCISE 5

BENCH-HOOK

Features presented:
Back-saw
Twist-bit
Brace
Hand-drill
Countersink
Screw-driver
Flat-head wood-screws

Figure 32 is the drawing of a bench-hook.

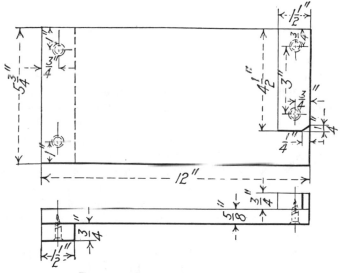

Fig. 32.—Drawing of a bench-hook.

A bench-hook is used, as illustrated in Fig. 33, to hold small pieces of wood, and to protect the bench while they are being

29

sawed or chisel pared.   It is made up of three pieces of wood;
the *plate D, cleat E,* and the *stop F*

The Back-saw.—The saw illustrated is known as the back-
saw; it is a fine-toothed *cross-cut saw* with the back of the blade

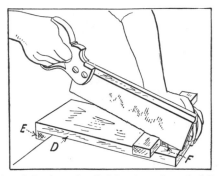

Fɪɢ. 33.—The bench-hook used to hold a piece of wood while it is being sawed
with a back-saw.

stiffened with a steel rib; it is the saw used for small bench
work.

In starting a saw cut, the saw should be guided by holding
the thumb of the left hand against the blade just above the
teeth.   The handle should be slightly raised so that the teeth
are in contact only at the farther edge of the wood, as shown.
As the sawing proceeds, the handle is gradually lowered until
the teeth are in contact across the
width of the piece.

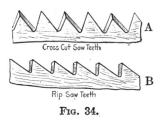

Fɪɢ. 34.

The *cross-cut saw* is used for sawing across the grain of wood; the
teeth are shaped as shown in
Fig. 34, A.   The *rip-saw* is used for
sawing in the direction of the grain
of wood; the teeth are shaped as
shown in Fig. 34, B.

Set.—Set is given the teeth of a saw so that the blade will
not *bind or wedge* in the cut.   Setting consists in *slightly bend-
ing* over every alternate tooth beyond the body of the blade.

The best way for a beginner to learn how to set and file a saw correctly is by *verbal instruction, careful supervision, and practice.*

The size of a saw is indicated by the *length* of the blade in inches. The size of the teeth is indicated by the *number* of *tooth-points* to the inch. The back-saw shown is a 10-inch 10-point back-saw.

The *cleat* and the *stop* of the bench-hook are secured to the plate with two 1¼-inch No. 10 flat-head wood-screws. The screws which secure the cleat to the plate *pass through* the cleat, and are screwed into the plate. The screws with which the stop is attached *pass through* the plate, and are screwed into the stop. By inserting the screws in this manner, the heads of the screws are exposed on the under side of the bench-hook only, and are out of the way of the *cutting-edge* of tools.

Flat-head Wood-screws.—Flat-head wood-screws are used for pattern work. The size of flat-head wood-screws is designated by their *length* over all in inches, and by *diameter* in number of the American screw-gage. They are specified as ¾ inch No. 8, 1½ inch No. 12, etc. They vary in size from ¼ inch No. 0 to 6 inch No. 30.

Below are the numbers of the screws chiefly used for pattern work, and the diameter of bit used for boring the hole for screws.

No. of screw	Diameter of screw, inch	Diameter of bit, inch
6	.1368	5⁄32
8	.1631	6⁄32
10	.1894	7⁄32
12	.2158	7⁄32
14	.2421	8⁄32
16	.2684	9⁄32

The selection of screws of the proper diameter is largely a matter of judgment. Their selection as to length will depend upon the thickness of the material through which the screw is to pass, and the length of *thread or hold* that may be obtained in the adjacent piece of wood.

When there is no reason for doing otherwise, *always* pass the screw through the material of the *lesser thickness* and screw it into the thicker. A screw driven parallel with the direction of the grain of wood (*in end grain wood*) does not have the *withdrawal* resistance that it will have if driven *transversely* to the direction of grain. Screws entering end grain wood should be screwed into the wood the *full length* of the threaded portion.

When two or more screws are used in the same locality, they should be so placed as to be out of the line of the same fiber of wood. Place screws as *far apart* as the work will permit.

When the thickness of the material will permit, the *threaded* portion of screws of 1¾ inches or less in length should be screwed into the wood. For screws of 2 or more inches in length, ¾ of the threaded portion of the screw will usually be found sufficient. If the thickness of the holding material will not permit these proportions, the *diameter* of the screw should be increased. Using a screw of a larger diameter will increase the withdrawal resistance. The advantage of screws is that they are strong and that they may be easily withdrawn and the work taken apart.

A cross section of two blocks, held together with a screw, is shown in Fig. 35. Attention is called to the *diameter* of the hole *I* in block *G*, and how the threaded portion of the screw is *screwed* into block *H*.

FIG. 35.—Two blocks secured together with a flat-head wood-screw.

When the material is too thick for the length of the screw at hand, or if it is desirable that the head of the screw be *set below* the surface as shown in Fig. 36, a hole is first bored (*counterbored*) to the required depth

R with an auger-bit of sufficient size to admit the head of the screw. The screw is then inserted in the usual way, and the hole closed by the insertion of plug *S*. A better appearing surface will result if the grain of wood of the plug lies in the same direction as the grain of the surrounding wood.

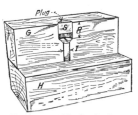

The insertion of a screw into *short grain* wood or near an edge is very apt to result in the splitting of the piece. To avoid this trouble, bore a hole (*pilot-hole*) of about the same *size* as that of the *root diameter* of the thread of the screw. The *root diam-*

Fig. 36.—Method of setting the head of a screw below the surface of the material.

eter of the thread is the diameter of the screw at the *bottom* of the thread. *Bore a pilot-hole for screws inserted into hard wood.* The mistake often made is the failure to bore the hole *I* large enough for the screw to slip through block *G* freely.

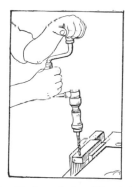

Fig. 37.—Boring a hole with a twist-bit held in a bit-brace.

Fig. 38.—The hand-drill.

The Bit-brace.—The bit-brace is used for boring, drilling and countersinking, and for driving and removing screws. The size of a brace is determined by the diameter of the circle *sweep* described by the throw of the crank.

2

Twist-bits.—Twist-bits are principally used for boring holes for screws.   Figure 37 illustrates the holes being bored with a twist-bit in the cleat *E* of the bench-stop.

A hole is more easily bored *perpendicular* to a surface if the piece is so placed or held that the surface lies in the *horizontal plane.*

The Hand-drill as shown in Fig. 38 is also used for boring holes for screws.   The chuck *K* is made to accomodate straight-shank bits or drills.

The Countersink.—To set a flat-head screw below the surface of the wood, the end of the hole requires a conical enlargement, or is *countersunk, as at J*, Fig. 35.   This is done with a *countersink* as shown at *L* Fig. 39.   The countersink is held in a brace.

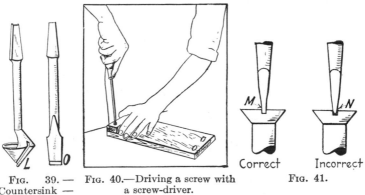

Correct   Incorrect

Fig.   39. —   Fig. 40.—Driving a screw with   Fig. 41.
Countersink —   a screw-driver.
Brace   s c r e w-
driver.

The Screw-driver.—The screw-driver as shown in Fig. 40, is used for turning the screw and driving it into the wood. Screw-drivers are made in various sizes.   It is very important that the point of the blade be so shaped (*of parallel thickness*) that it correctly fits the slot of the screw, as shown at *M*, Fig. 41.   If the point of the blade be ground wedge-shape, as shown at *N*, the blade will tend to come out of the slot when turned. Exert a good end pressure on the handle when driving a screw.

The screw-driver, as shown at *O*, Fig. 39, is held in a brace. Stock required: ¾ × 6 × 12½ inches, plate ⅞ × 1¾ × 11 inches, cleat and stop

ORDER OF OPERATIONS

1. Dress plate *D* to the required thickness, length and width.
2. Plane material for the cleat *E* and the stop *F* to the required thickness and width.
3. Saw (*use back-saw*) the cleat and the stop to the required length. Chamfer the corner of the stop *F* as shown in Fig. 32.
4. Locate, bore and countersink the screw holes in the plate.
5. Locate, bore and countersink the screw holes in the cleat.
6. *Before attaching*, place parts together in their correct relation to each other, then compare the work with the drawing, and *mark* their position.
7. Attach parts.

QUESTIONS

1. For what purpose is a bench-hook used?
2. What is understood by a cross-cut saw?
3. What is understood by a rip-saw?
4. What is understood by the expression "set" as applied to a saw?
5. How is the size of a saw blade indicated?
6. How is the size of saw teeth indicated?
7. How is the size of flat-head screws indicated?
8. What is the advantage of screws over nails?
9. Describe the operations necessary to secure two pieces of wood together with a wood-screw.
10. For what purpose is a countersink used?
11. What is understood by counterbore as applied to holes for screws?
12. What is the object in boring a pilot-hole for a screw?
13. Why should a screw driven in the direction of the grain of the wood have a greater amount of grip than if driven in a transverse direction to the grain?
14. When two or more screws are used in the same locality, how should they be placed?

15. Why should the screw hole through a piece to be attached with a screw be of such diameter as to freely admit the screw?

16. When the material is too thick for the screw at hand, what is the usual procedure?

17. How should the point of a screw-driver blade be ground?

18. Why should the parts of the bench-hook be placed in position and compared with the drawing before being attached together?

19. How is the size of a bit-brace specified?

20. What is understood by the term root diameter of a screw?

21. What is gained by inserting the screws through the plate and the cleat of the bench-hook as described?

PATTERN 1

PLATE

Features presented:

Draft	Contraction
A green sand mold	Sandpapering patterns
Shrinkage of metal	Shellacking patterns

Figure 42 is the drawing of a cast iron plate.

Draft.—To assist in the removal of a pattern from the sand, a slight slant, called *draft*, is given those surfaces of the pattern

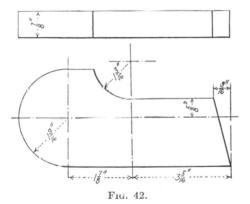

Fig. 42.

which *parallel* the direction in which the pattern is *drawn*. *Drawing* a pattern, is the operation of pulling or removing it from the sand.

It is therefore necessary that the surfaces requiring draft be determined by the *molding position* of the pattern. This is clearly illustrated by the rectangular casting and the patterns shown in Fig. 43. The pattern may be molded in three different positions.

37

For the sake of clearness, the *draft* upon the surfaces of the patterns in the illustration is greatly exaggerated. Illustration *A*, calls attention to the surfaces and the direction of the *draft* if the pattern is molded *flat-wise; B*, if the pattern is molded *edge-wise;* and *C*, if molded *end-wise.*

The *molding position* of a pattern is determined by the *size, shape* and the *requirement* of the casting. These features

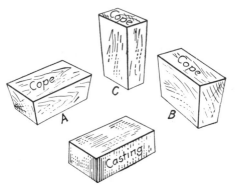

FIG. 43.—Patterns for a block casting illustrating how the molding position of the pattern determines the arrangement of the draft.

will be described as the patterns which embody them are given consideration.

Draw is the depth to which a pattern is embedded in the sand.

The general practice followed is to arrange a pattern to mold in the position which requires the *least draw.* The application of this feature is made to the pattern under consideration.

Draft is to be *added* to the dimensions given on the drawing. By adding the draft, the parting or cope surface of the pattern is *made larger.*

The cope surface of a pattern is bounded by that line about a pattern where the parting in the mold is made. Unless otherwise instructed, ⅟₆₄ *inch draft to* 1 *inch of draw* will be allowed on external surfaces.

A Green Sand Mold.—This book is not intended to teach foundry practice, but as pattern-making precedes and supplements this art, it is necessary to take up the elementary principles of *molding* which will tend to show the reason for embodying certain *features in pattern construction.*

The most common mold (*green sand mold*) is formed by ramming damp molding sand about a pattern contained in a surrounding frame or box called a *flask.* The impression of the pattern is retained by reason of the dampness.

FIG. 44.—The relative postions of the drag and cope sections of a two part flask and the bottom board.

An impression is taken from the pattern and the pattern then withdrawn from the sand. To accomplish this, a mold is divided or made up of two or more sections.

When of two sections, it consists of a *drag* or bottom section, and a *cope* or top section. The relative positions of the cope, drag and bottom-board is shown in Fig. 44.

To permit the sections of a mold being separated, then later of being replaced in their correct relation, the flask is fitted with pins and sockets.

The joint or surface, which separates two sections of a mold, is called *the parting.* The surface of a pattern exposed when the cope is lifted off, is called the *parting or cope surface,* (*cope face*). The surface of a pattern which leaves its impression in the sand of the drag is called the *drag surface,* (*drag face*).

The first operation in the process of mold making is to place the drag upon the mold-board, then place the pattern in the desired position, (*cope face down*) upon the board.

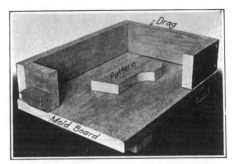

Fig. 45.—First step in the process of mold making.

Figure 45 illustrates the work at this stage. A section of one side and end of the flask has been cut away. This makes possible the view of the pattern upon the mold board. The

Fig. 46.—The second step in the process of mold making.

flask is now ready to receive the sand, which is rammed to the top edge of the flask and struck off level with a straight-edge. The bottom-board (*a board similar to the mold-board*) is now placed upon this surface, the two boards held tight against the flask, and the work *rolled over*. The mold-board is now removed.

The second step in the making of the mold is illustrated in Fig. 46. The parting has been prepared, the sprue-pin set and the cope in place ready to receive and be rammed up with sand. The *sprue-pin* forms an opening through the sand of the cope into which the metal is poured.

After the cope is rammed up and lifted off, the pattern is drawn. *Drawing* the pattern is done with the aid of a draw

Fig. 47.—The mold ready to be closed.

spike and by slightly *rapping* the pattern to *loosen it* from the sand. Figure 47 illustrates the mold completed and ready to be closed. To conduct the metal from the sprue to the impression left by the pattern, a *gate* is cut in the parting of the drag, as shown.

Shrinkage.—During the changing of metal from a solid to a liquid state through the action of heat, it *expands*. When allowed to cool a reverse action, termed *shrinkage* takes place. The term *shrinkage* as applied to metal is understood to mean the arranging or changing of the structure of the metal during the cooling period.

Contraction as applied to metal refers to the amount *per foot* that the metal through the action of shrinkage decreases in bulk between the time it is poured and the time when it has cooled to normal temperature.

It will be readily seen that if the pattern were made the *required size* of the object, the casting made from it would be found *under-size* an amount equal to the *contraction*.   In order to compensate for the decrease in size of the casting, it is necessary to make the pattern *larger* by this amount.

If the standard rule were used in dimensioning patterns, it would be necessary when laying out the work to calculate and allow for the contraction.   This is eliminated by the use of a contraction-rule.

A contraction-rule is *a rule so graduated that it maintains an exact contraction relation between all dimensions.*

The various metals do not contract alike, and for this reason it becomes necessary to have rules varying in contraction allowance.   For instance, cast-iron will usually contract $\frac{1}{10}$ inch to 1 foot in length.   Brass or bronze, $\frac{5}{32}$ of an inch; steel castings will contract $\frac{2}{10}$ inch to 1 foot; aluminum, $\frac{1}{4}$ inch per foot.   Contraction may be disregarded in small patterns, as the rapping of a pattern will enlarge the mold sufficiently to compensate for this decreasing action.

Graduating a Contraction Rule.—Figure 48 illustrates a method by which a contraction rule may be graduated from a

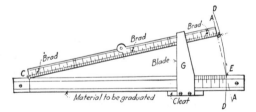

Fig. 48.—Graduating a contraction rule from a standard rule.

standard rule.   If the transferring of lines is carefully done, the contraction rule thus made will be found accurate enough for most purposes.

Secure the standard rule to a board with small brads driven in flush with the face of the rule   At one end scribe perpendicular to the edge of the rule, the line *AA*.   From the end of the rule lay off as indicated by *B*, the amount of contraction to be allowed in 2 feet. With C as the center and with a radius equal to the length of the standard rule plus the contraction amount B, scribe an arc D, intersecting the perpendicular line AA at E.

The material to be graduated is then secured to the board in the position shown, its inner edge passing through the point of intersection at E. The transfer of lines is made with the aid of a hardwood blade, G. The attached cleat permits it to be used like a tee-square.

Figure 49 shows how the shape of *the pattern will appear when laid out upon the material.*

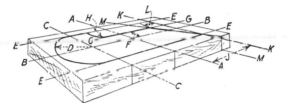

FIG. 49.—The shape of the plate pattern laid out upon the material.

Draft is required on those surfaces of a pattern which parallel the direction in which it is drawn from the sand. *The edge surfaces* of the plate pattern *lie* in this direction and therefore will receive this consideration.

Stock required: $1 \times 3\frac{1}{2} \times 7\frac{1}{2}$ inches.

ORDER OF OPERATIONS

1. Prepare the material.

2. Scribe center line A at the middle of its length, and gage line B along the middle of its width.

3. From center line A locate and scribe the center line C.

4. Select one face and mark it the *cope face;* mark the opposite face the *drag face.*

Draft enlarges a pattern toward the parting, or the *cope face;* therefore the shape of the drag face of the pattern will be laid out to the *given dimensions on the drawing.* One sixty-fourth of an inch will be allowed for *draft* upon the edge surfaces of the pattern.

5. With the intersection of the lines *B* and *C* as a center, using the *radius D*, scribe upon the *drag face* a semicircumference. Increase *radius D* $\frac{1}{64}$ inch and repeat the operation on the *cope face*.

6. Gage the lines *EE* tangent to the semicircumference.

7. Lay off the dimension represented by *F* and gage the line *G*. Add $\frac{1}{64}$ inch to the *dimension F* and repeat the operation on the *cope face*.

8. Locate the center of the radius *H* upon the line *A* and scribe an arc tangent to line *G*.

Note.—It is unnecessary to make any change in the radius *H* for draft allowance, when scribing this arc upon the cope face of the pattern. The draft allowance made upon the surface represented by the line *G* automatically shifts the center of the arc, and gives the draft allowance upon this concave surface.

9. Lay off the dimension represented by *J* and scribe the line *K* across the drag face.

10. Lay off upon line *G* the dimension represented by *L*. Then scribe the line *M* which represents the *angle* this end of the pattern forms with the *center line B*.

11. From the points where line *M* intersects the edge corners of the material, scribe lines across the two edge surfaces. Scribe lightly line *M* across the *cope face*, connecting the points.

12. Make draft allowance $\frac{1}{64}$ inch for end surface and scribe this line parallel to light line *M*.

13. Saw and dress the work to shape. (*Refer to the instructions on chisel and gouge-paring given with the Exercises.*)

Sandpapering Patterns.—*All tool work* is to be completed, then the work is to be sandpapered. *This direction* is to be followed until instructions are given to the contrary.

Before a pattern receives its protective coating of shellac, it is sandpapered in order to remove the ridges and marks left by the tools. Cabinet work requires that sandpapering be done in the direction of the grain of wood. Sandpapering patterns may be done with or across the grain.

Sandpaper (garnet paper) is graded numerically from fine to coarse, as follows: No. 0000, 000, 00, 0, ½, 1½, 2, 2½. Of these grades, No. 0, ½, 1, are generally used for pattern work.

A coarse grade may be first used, and later the surface further smoothed down by the use of a finer grade. The best results are obtained by using the sandpaper over a *soft wood block*.

For flat surfaces, hold the block down firmly, passing it back and forth without releasing the pressure. Illustration

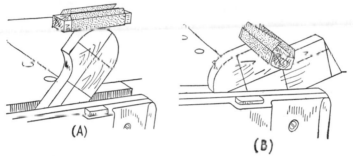

Method of sand papering the convex edge surface of the plate pattern.

Method of sand papering the concave edge surface of the plate pattern.

Figs. 50, A and 50, B.

Fig. 50, A shows how the block is held when sandpapering the *convex* surface of the pattern. Illustration B shows how the face of the block is *dressed to conform* to the *concave* surface of the pattern. This surface requires an oscillating movement of the block.

Always sandpaper an edge surface in the direction of its length; if done across the edge, the finished surface will likely be *found convexed*.

Shellacking Patterns.—Patterns are given a coating of shellac to *seal* the pores of wood and prevent as far as possible *swelling* and *warping* caused by the absorption of moisture from the sand.

Shellac, or what is known as Lac in its native state, is the joint product of a scale insect and the juice of trees. The shellac used for pattern work is known as *yellow or orange shellac.*

Shellac varnish or shellac is a solution of shellac gum in either denatured alcohol or wood alcohol. Both of the latter are poisonous to drink.

Shellac sets very quickly, due to the rapid evaporation of the alcohol.

Thin shellac about the consistency of machine oil, should be used.

The number of coats depends upon the protection desired. Two coats may be regarded as a minimum, and four as a maximum.

See that the surface is free from *dust*, then apply the shellac *evenly* and *quickly*. Take up very little shellac on the brush; *avoid* going over the surface more times than is required to cover it.

Always pass the brush from the work, for if passed in the opposite direction, the edge of the object will wipe some shellac from the brush, and it will run down over this surface. The result will be an uneven surface, detracting from the appearance of the pattern and adding to the difficulties of *drawing it.*

Shellac can be spread a little more uniformly if done in the direction of the grain of the wood instead of across it. However, the shape of the pattern will determine the manner of applying.

Shellac is apparently dry after a few moments, but to get the best results, the pattern should be left for about *an hour or more* before handling.

The surface, when dry, and especially after the first coat, will feel rough. This roughness is due to the alcohol causing a slight raising of the wood's grain. This roughness should be smoothed down with used, or very fine sandpaper. The process of sandpapering and shellacking should be *repeated* until the desired number of coats has been applied.

Dissolving or Cutting Shellac.—Shellac gum and alcohol, in the proportions of about 3 pounds of shellac to 1 gallon of alcohol, are put into a receptacle which can be tightly closed, and, with occasional stirring, left for several hours to dissolve. If found too thick for use, the shellac is thinned by adding alcohol.

Shellac is best kept in a *glass or earthen* container. Shellac is *discolored* through contact with metal.

The shellac container should be so arranged that the brush is suspended as to permit of about ½ or 1 inch of the bristles to be immersed in the shellac. If the weight of the brush is allowed to rest upon the bristles, the bristles will become *bent and the usefulness of the brush impaired.*

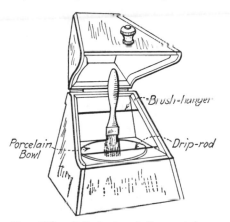

Fig. 50C.—Self-closing shellac container.

Figure 50C illustrates a type of container which has been found very practical. The joint between the hinged cover and the reservoir is so shaped that it gives free access to the shellac and also permits the brush to be suspended as shown. The handle upon the back of the container and not in view, acts as a stop and causes the cover, upon its release, to drop down into place.

A small amount of oxalic acid placed in the shellac will improve its clearness and color.

Shellac is *colored* by adding coloring matter. If pigment is used, it should first be *mixed* in alcohol, then added to the shellac, and thoroughly mixed by stirring.   The use of colored shellac is a matter of choice.

QUESTIONS

1. What is understood by the term founding or foundry practice?

2. What is a foundry mold?

3. What is understood by the term pattern-making?

4. What is a foundry pattern?

5. Why is a thorough knowledge of the principles of mechanical drawing and foundry practice necessary to become a successful pattern-maker?

6. Why is it that a model of an object cannot always be used as a pattern?

7. What is understood by the term draft as applied to a pattern?

8. What surfaces of a pattern require draft?

9. What determines the surfaces to be drafted?

10. What determines the molding position of a pattern?

11. What is understood by the cope surface of a pattern?

12. When a mold is made up of two sections, how are the sections designated?

13. What is understood by the parting of a mold?

14. What is understood by the drag face of a pattern?

15. Describe the various operations required in making the mold for the plate pattern.

16. Why is the plate pattern molded flatwise?

17. What is a sprue-pin?

18. What is understood by the term gate as applied to a mold?

19. What is understood by rapping a pattern?

20. What is understood by the term drawing a pattern?

21. Define contraction.

22. Define shrinkage.

23. Explain the difference between the standard rule and a contraction-rule.

24. What is understood by the parting line of a pattern?

25. Why may the contraction in small patterns be disregarded?

26. Make a sketch, and explain how a contraction-rule may be graduated from a standard rule.

27. Give the reason for sandpapering the surfaces of a pattern.

28. How does sandpapering patterns differ from sandpapering cabinet-work?

29. How should sandpaper be used to obtain the best result?

30. Why should narrow edge surfaces be sandpapered in the direction of their length?

PATTERN 2

WASHER

Features presented:
A green sand core
Draft on the walls of small holes and openings
Sandpapering small interior conical surfaces
Figure 51 is the drawing of a cast iron washer.

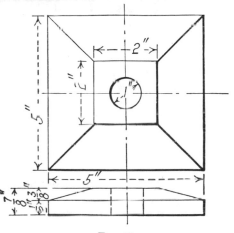

FIG. 51.

The word *core* as applied to a mold is understood as meaning that part of the mold or body of sand which is to form a *hole, a cavity, or an interior opening* in a casting.

The open mold as shown in Fig. 52 illustrates this feature. The letter *A* designates the *core*. It is that part of the mold, or body of sand, which was delivered by the hole in the pattern.

4   49

Excess draft is given the wall of a hole to release the core with the least disturbance. *Failure* to allow this excess draft upon such surfaces is likely to cause the core to be broken from the adjoining sand and lifted out with the pattern.

Fig. 52.—The washer mold.

One thirty second of an inch to 1 inch of *draw* is to be allowed upon the wall of holes, unless otherwise instructed. It is assumed that a hole in a casting is to receive a bolt or bar. Therefore, the given dimension of the hole *must not be made less* by the addition of draft to its wall.

The size of the hole at the parting surface is made to the dimension on the drawing, the draft *enlarging* it toward the drag face. The shape of the washer suggests that the pattern be molded flat-wise, with the impression of the chamfered face formed in the drag.

Stock required: $1 \times 5\frac{1}{2} \times 5\frac{1}{2}$ inches

ORDER OF OPERATIONS

1. Prepare the material.

2. The washer being of rectangular form, the material will be dressed to the over-all length and width dimension of the pattern. The draft allowance on the edge surfaces will not be laid out, but these surfaces are to receive this *consideration*.

3. Scribe and gage lines *A* and *B* upon one face, Fig. 53.

4. Square the lines across the edge surfaces and scribe and gage lines *A* and *B* upon the opposite face.

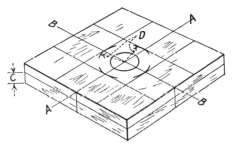

FIG. 53.—The construction lines of the drag face of the washer pattern as they are to appear upon the material.

5. Gage upon the edges the dimension represented by *C*.

6. From the intersection of the center lines *A* and *B*, scribe upon the *cope face* a circumference which is the given diameter of the bolt-hole. Provide *draft* upon the wall of the hole by enlarging the radius $\frac{1}{32}$ inch, and scribe a circumference upon the *drag face*.

7. To establish the angle of the chamfered surface, set the dividers to 1 inch, then from the intersection of the center lines, scribe arcs *D* as shown.

8. Lines scribed and gaged tangent to these arcs will complete the layout of the pattern.

Figure 53 shows how the construction lines of the pattern *are to appear upon drag face when completed and the work ready for the dressing out of the bolt-hole.*

Verify all the dimensions of the pattern with those on the drawing.

9. Locate a $\frac{7}{8}$-inch *auger-bit* at the intersection of the center lines and bore a hole. There is less danger of *splitting* the wood if the hole is bored from each face to the center of the thickness.

Auger-bits.—Auger-bits are made in many styles. The most common form is shown in Fig. 54. They are made in sizes advancing by sixteenths of an inch from ³⁄₁₆ inch up. The size of an auger-bit is given in sixteenths. The size is stamped in one of the flat surfaces of the shank.

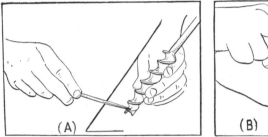 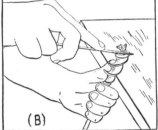

FIG. 54A.—Filing the lip of an auger-bit. FIG. 54B.—Filing the spur of an auger-bit.

Sharpening an auger-bit. The lip of an auger-bit is sharpened with a file as shown in Fig. 54, A. *Never file* the lip on the under side, for this is liable to change the angle and thereby impair its cutting efficiency.

The spur is sharpened as shown in Fig. 54, B. Use the file on the inside of the spur only. An auger-bit should never be *filed* on the outside. Any roughness caused by filing the spurs should be removed by laying the bit upon an oil-stone and *revolving it*.

The Expansion-bit.—The expansion-bit shown in Fig. 55, A has an adjustable spur and lip. It is designed to bore holes of different diameters.

(A)   (B)

FIG. 55A. Expansion bit.   FIG. 55B. Bit-file.

The Bit-file.—The bit-file, as shown in Fig. 55, B, is designed for sharpening auger-bits. Its cutting and shape adapt it to filing the lips and spurs.

10. Pare the hole to size.

11. Chamfer the face of the pattern, then draft the edges.

Tapered holes are best sandpapered with the aid of a *conical form*, as shown in Fig. 56. *Refer to the information given with Exercise* 7. By inserting one corner of the paper in the

FIG. 56.—Sandpaper-roll.

saw-cut and wrapping the paper around as shown, a conical sandpaper surface is made. A *rotary* movement is given to the form while sandpapering.

Finish the surfaces of the pattern with shellac, then number the pattern. The number of a pattern is *never* to be stamped *in a surface* which lies *parallel* to the direction the pattern is drawn. A number stamped in such surfaces will *interfere* with the drawing of the pattern.

QUESTIONS

1. Why are patterns given a coating of shellac?
2. Of what is shellac composed?
3. What solvent is used for shellac?
4. Why should a vessel containing shellac be kept closed?
5. What should be avoided when applying shellac?
6. Why should sandpapering the surface precede each coat of shellac?
7. What is understood by the term, cutting shellac?
8. Why is the use of thin shellac more satisfactory than thick?
9. Why is shellac best kept in an earthen or glass container?
10. What chemical placed in shellac will improve its color?
11. How is colored shellac produced?
12. What is a core?
13. Why is excess draft given the walls of small holes?
14. Why should the draft upon the walls enlarge the given dimension of the hole toward the drag face of the pattern?
15. What is an auger-bit?
16. What part of an auger-bit is the lip? What part is the spur?
17. What function does the lead-screw perform?
18. What is understood by the mean diameter of the lead-screw?
19. What may be done to prevent the lead-screw of an auger-bit from splitting the wood?

MACHINE-FINISH

Machine-finish is the operation of removing or cutting from a casting an amount of stock, in order to produce a *finished surface*.

FIG. 57.—Finishing the surface of the platen casting.

Figure 57 illustrates one of the machine tools which may be used when finishing a flat surface of a casting. The letter A designates the cutting tool, B the thickness of the metal (*finish allowance*) being removed.

The drawing gives the *finished* dimensions of a casting. The *pattern-maker* is to add to those surfaces indicated by the word *"finish,"* or *finish mark* "*F*," *finish allowance*, that the *casting may be machined to the given size.*

One eighth of an inch finish allowance will be allowed on the surfaces of *cast iron or steel*, unless otherwise instructed.

One sixteenth of an inch finish allowance will be allowed on the surface of brass or aluminum unless otherwise instructed.

PATTERN 3

PLATEN

Features presented:
Machine-finish
Finish allowance for cast-iron
Drilled holes
Sandpapering small interior concave surfaces.
Figure 58 is the drawing of a cast iron platen.

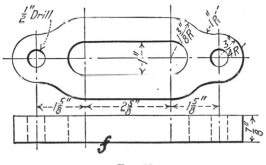

FIG. 58.

A finish mark F appears on the line which represents the edge, the only visible part of the surface of the platen requiring *machine-finish*. This means that instead of the platen pattern being made to the thickness given on the drawing, ⅞ inch, the thickness is increased (⅛ inch) by the amount which has been allowed for the operation, *machine-finish*.

The ½-inch holes shown near the ends of the casting are specified to be drilled. This means that the holes are to be made in the casting by a metal-cutting tool known as a drill. *No consideration* is to be given holes which are less than 1¼ inches in diameter, unless otherwise instructed.

55

The platen pattern will be molded flat-wise.

Figure 59 illustrates the shape of the pattern laid out upon the material.

Stock required $1\frac{1}{8} \times 3 \times 7\frac{1}{8}$ inches.

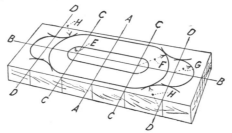

FIG. 59.—The construction lines of the platen pattern as they are to appear upon both faces of the material.

ORDER OF OPERATIONS

1. Prepare the material and locate the center lines A and B.

2. From line A lay off and scribe lines C and C.

Dimensions are to be laid off from a base line. On this pattern, lines C are to be located from the base line A. The center lines D are to be located from the base line A. *Under no circumstances would the center lines D be located from the center lines C.*

3. Mark one face, cope, the opposite face, drag.

4. Upon the *cope face*, lay out the width of the slot by scribing semicircumferences, using a radius equal to E. Make the *draft* allowance, and repeat the operation upon the *drag face*.

5. Upon the *drag face* lay out the width of the pattern by scribing semicircumferences using a radius equal to F. Make the *draft* allowance and repeat the operation upon the *cope face*.

6. Upon the *drag face*, lay out the semicircular ends of the pattern by scribing semicircumferences, using a radius equal to G. Make the draft allowance and repeat the operation upon the *cope face*. Upon the cope and drag faces scribe arcs tangent to the semicircumferences already drawn, using a radius equal to H.

7. Remove waste from the slot by *boring* a series of ⅞-inch holes tangent to one another.

The *lead-screw* of a ⅞-inch auger-bit is apt to *split* the wood when holes are bored so close together. Splitting is *avoided* by first boring holes (*pilot holes*), whose diameter is about equal to the mean diameter of the lead screw.

The mean diameter of the lead-screw of an auger-bit, is the diameter of the screw at the *middle* of its length.

8. Saw and dress the edge surface to shape.

Fig. 60.—Method of sandpapering the concave surfaces of the slot in the platen pattern.

Small interior concave surfaces are best sandpapered with the aid of a cylindrical form or roll, as shown in Fig. 60. The roll is given a rotary movement. (*Refer to information on sandpapering given with Pattern 1.*)

PATTERN 4

SURFACE-PLATE

Features presented:
  The names of the parts or members of a casting
  Requirements of a casting which determine the molding
    position of the pattern
  Coping out
  Draft allowance on coped surfaces
  Built-up patterns
  The butt-joint
  Glue
  Wire brads
  The trimmer
  Leather fillets
  Beeswax
Figure 61 is the drawing of a cast iron surface-plate.

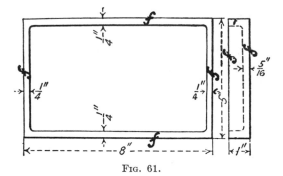

Fig. 61.

There are certain more or less well-defined names applied to the *parts or members* which go to make up a casting. For instance, a wheel is made up of a hub, the arms or spokes, and

58

the rim. The surface-plate is made up of a *web A* and a *flange B*.

The shape of the casting would suggest that the flange side of the pattern be molded in the drag, but the following reason shows why the pattern is molded in the *reverse position*.

Any slag, sand or gas, trapped in the molten metal, rises to the top, giving a *coarse and poorer grain* to the casting at this point. Iron is more dense and free from impurities at the *bottom* of the mold. It is very important that the metal in the flat side of a surface plate be *dense and free from impurities*. Therefore, the flat side of the pattern is molded in the drag or at the *bottom* of the mold.

The inside surfaces of the flange of the casting are formed by the sand of the cope extending below the parting of the mold, as indicated by *C* in Fig. 62. When the sand of the

Fig. 62.—The surface plate mold. The pattern is shown in place.

cope extends down and takes the impression of the pattern, as in this case, it is said to be *coped out*.

A surface of a pattern which lies vertical to the parting of the mold and is to be coped, must be given *excess draft*. Excess draft is to facilitate the lifting out of the projecting body of sand. *One sixteenth of an inch draft to each inch of depth*, is to be allowed upon such surfaces, unless otherwise instructed.

When patterns assume such form and proportion that it would not be practicable to work them out of one piece of wood, they are *built up*, the joints between the adjacent pieces of wood depending upon *glue* and *brads* to hold them together.

The butt-joint is the most common joint used in pattern construction, the adjoining pieces of wood being placed or butted together and secured with glue, brads or screws. The *butt-joint* is used in the construction of the surface-plate pattern.

Glue—Its Preparation and Use.—Glue, as used for pattern work, is known as animal glue, the best grade being obtained from hides. The essentials for a good glue joint are: *true surfaces, a good grade of glue, and its proper preparation for use.*

Glue in a dry state will keep indefinitely, but when once prepared for use, it deteriorates rapidly, hence a greater amount of glue than is likely to be used for two or possibly three days ahead, should not be prepared at one time.

To prepare for use, it should be placed in a kettle, covered with cold water, and allowed to soak until it jellies. It should then be heated over boiling water until perfectly fluid.

After glue has been thoroughly heated, the temperature of the water should be slightly reduced below the boiling point, as the excessive heating of glue only lessens its *adhesive qualities.*

Caution.—*Dry heat* should never be applied directly to the vessel containing the glue, as it will scorch or burn, and become *unfit* for use.

Glue should always be heated in a double or water jacketed kettle. The inner kettle contains the glue; the outer kettle is the water reservoir. By this arrangement, the glue does not come in direct contact with the source of heat, but in turn is *heated* by the water.

Do not prepare glue in a kettle containing any old glue. Boil out the kettle before putting a new supply to soak. The consistency of glue for general use should be *comparatively thin. Hot water* should be used for thinning glue.

If the glue is *chilled* or used too *thick*, no amount of pressure will bring the surfaces of wood into contact. *Contact of the surfaces of the wood is absolutely essential to a strong glue joint.*

End grain wood is so porous that if glue is applied directly to a surface, it is *absorbed* and conducted away before it has time to set. This may be overcome by giving the surface a primary coat of very *thin* glue; this is called *sizing.* When the sizing has thoroughly dried, the joint is glued in the usual way. A joint between end grain wood is not as strong as that between length grain, and should *never be relied upon unless reinforced.*

Wire Brads.—The common wire brad is chiefly used for small and medium size pattern work. The smallness of the head permits them to be set below the surface of wood with the least defacement.

The length of brads is given in inches, and the wire gage or diameter, in number—usually expressed 1¼ inch No. 17, etc. Their selection as to length will depend upon the thickness of material they are to secure, and the depth of grip or holding surface that may be obtained in the adjacent piece of wood.

When the thickness of the material will permit, the *length of grip* should at least equal one half the length of the brad. If the thickness of the holding material will not allow this proportion, the brad should then be *toed, or driven in obliquely,* to secure sufficient withdrawal resistance.

When the case permits, drive the brad through the material of the *lesser* thickness, into the *thicker.* A brad driven parallel to the direction of the grain of wood (*in end grain wood*) does not have the withdrawal resistance that it will have if it is driven *at an angle* to the direction of the grain.

Place brads as far apart as the work will permit. Strength does not depend so much upon the number of brads, *as upon how they are placed.* When two or more brads are used in the same locality, they should be so placed (*staggered*) as to be out of the line of the same fibre of the wood.

Driving a brad through a piece of short grain wood is likely to *split* it; therefore use the brad as a drill point in a hand-drill, and bore a *pilot-hole*, then insert the brad and drive it home.

Do not drive the head of a brad down flush with the surface of the wood, but allow it to slightly protrude, then use a *nail-set* as shown in Fig. 63.

Do not forget that the point of nail-sets vary in size.

Do not leave the head of a brad exposed, but set the head below the surface and fill the depression with wax or putty.

Brads should never be used except when they can be so placed as to be in no danger of contact with the tools. Brads are used to good advantage in hastening the work, because they take the place of hand screws while the glue is setting.

FIG. 63. Nail-set.

The following sizes are those mostly used for pattern work:

½ inch No. 20	1½ inch No. 15
⅝ inch No. 19	1¾ inch No. 14
¾ inch No. 18	2 inch No. 14
1 inch No. 17	2½ inch No. 13
1¼ inch No. 16	3 inch No. 12

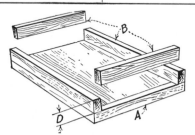

FIG. 64.—Attaching the flange material to the web.

The common flat-head or wire nail is used when greater withdrawal resistance is desired and the largeness of head is not objectionable.

Figure 64 illustrates the *surface-plate pattern* in course of construction. The web, as indicated by *A*, is the flat portion of the casting. The flange is indicated by *B*; it is the projection about the outer edge of the web.

Stock required: 9/16 × 5½ × 8¾ inches Web

⅞ × 1⅜ × 13½ inches Flange

ORDER OF OPERATIONS

1. Dress the web material to thickness, width and length. (*Note surfaces to be finished, then refer to information on machine finish Page 53.*)

Two pieces of flange stock are made from one piece of material as shown in Fig. 65. One of these pieces makes one side and *one* end flange.

FIG. 65.—Flange stock in process of shaping.

2. Dress the flange material to required thickness *D* Fig. 64, then square each edge.

3. From each edge, gage upon one face the thickness *E* of flange; *add draft allowance to E*, and repeat the operation upon the opposite face.

4. Separate the material along the middle of its width and plane the flange stock to its diminishing thickness.

5. Attach the flange as shown in Fig. 64 along the width of the web with *glue* and *three 1-inch brads*. *Glue should always be used* when attaching pattern parts.

6. Fit the end flanges in between the side flanges.

The Trimmer.—The trimmer as shown in Fig. 66 is used for dressing or trimming *end grain wood only*, and is the tool

best adapted for this work.   The gages *G* may be set at any
desired angle, and secured in position by the clamp *H*.   *Always*
hold the material firmly against the face of the *bed* and face
of the *gage*.

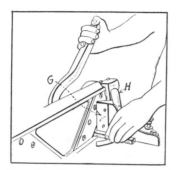

FIG. 66.—Dressing the flange stock
to length upon the trimmer.

The end flanges, are shown
above the surface of the web to
which they are to be attached
with *glue* and *two* 1-inch brads.
The joints between the side and
end flanges are to be reinforced
with *one* 1¼-inch brad.

7. Draft the edge surfaces of
the pattern.   *Refer to the illustration of the mold*, Fig. 62.

8. Fillet the corners of the
pattern.   One-eighth inch leather
fillet will be used.

Leather Fillets.—While the avoidance of sharp corners adds
greatly to the appearance of a casting, the real benefit derived
is the *added strength* given to the casting.   Further, the fillet-
ing of corners eliminates *sharp edges* of sand, so likely to be
loosened by the rapping of the pattern and to subsequently
fall into the mold.

Of the many kinds of material from which fillet stock is
made, *leather* is recognized as giving the *best result*.   The
pliability of leather makes this kind of fillet the most approved,
as it readily conforms to irregular shapes.   Added pliability
is obtained by *moistening* the face of the fillet.

Glue is used to affix leather fillets.   The method of procedure is to cut the fillet stock to the necessary lengths, then
place the fillet face down upon a board and apply the glue.   It
is then laid in position and rubbed into place by means of a
fillet iron.

Fillet-iron.—The fillet-iron is shown in Fig. 67.   *Immedi-
ately remove* with a damp cloth any surplus glue squeezed
out along the edges.

Leather fillet stock ranges in size from $\frac{1}{16}$-inch radius to 1-inch radius. For the ordinary run of small machine castings, $\frac{1}{8}$- $\frac{1}{4}$- and $\frac{3}{8}$-inch fillets are chiefly used.

FIG. 67.—Fillet-iron, used for rubbing leather fillets into place.

Beeswax is used for small fillets and to fill up holes made by brads and screws. It is worked into place with a fillet-iron. The iron is *heated* just enough to make the wax *impressible* but not to melt it. Wax fillet is worked into place after a pattern surface has received the *first* coat of shellac.

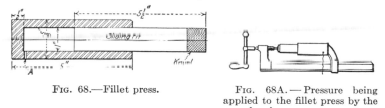

FIG. 68.—Fillet press.   FIG. 68A. — Pressure being applied to the fillet press by the use of a clamp.

A simple device for making wax fillet is shown in Fig. 68. The cylinder, *slightly heated*, is partially filled with shaved wax; pressure then applied to the end of the plunger Fig. 68A. will cause the wax to issue from the hole A in an unbroken thread. For fillets of $\frac{1}{8}$-inch radius, make the hole A $\frac{1}{16}$-inch diameter.

QUESTIONS

1. How is the size of auger-bits specified?
2. What is an expansion-bit?
3. What part of an auger-bit is the shank?
4. Why is a bit-file especially adapted to filing auger-bits?
5. Why should the lip of an auger-bit never be filed on the under side?
6. Why should the inside only, of the spur be filed?
7. How should any roughness on the outside of the spur be removed?
8. How is the wall of small conical shaped holes best sandpapered?
9. What is machine-finish?

5

10. What is finish allowance?

11. How does a drawing indicate that the surface of a casting is required to be finished?

12. What amount of finish allowance is usually provided upon the surface of cast iron?

13. How are small interior concave surfaces best sandpapered?

14. What are the names of the members which go to make up the surface-plate?

15. Why should the face of the surface-plate be cast downward or at the bottom of the mold?

16. What is understood by coping out?

17. Why should the surface of a pattern which lies vertical to the parting and is coped, be given excess draft?

18. Describe a butt-joint.

PATTERN 5

CLAMP

Features presented:
Vertical dry sand core
Core-print
The bevel
The protractor
The firmer-gouge
Shellacking core-prints
Marking the location of the core on the pattern when
the core comes just to the surface of a casting
Figure 69 is the drawing of a cast iron clamp.

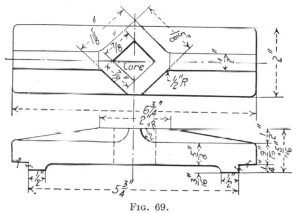

FIG. 69.

The pattern for the clamp is shown in Fig. 70. The casting
is composed of the *plate A,* a rectangular *pad B,* and the two
ribs C. A rectangular hole is to pass through the casting.
This requires the application of a *dry sand core.*

Cores.—A core is shown in the illustration of the washer
mold Fig. 52, page 50. *The core* indicated by *A* is the conical

67

body of sand delivered by the hole in the pattern. It is called *a green sand core*, because it is made of *green (damp) sand*.

The shape of green sand bodies are retained only by reason of the *dampness*. Therefore the *size* and *shape* of the core and *metal thickness* through which a *vertical green sand* core is to pass, will determine its application.

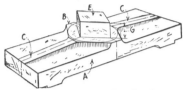

FIG. 70.—The pattern for the clamp.

The following is a safe rule to apply to a vertical green sand core: If the core is round, *the diameter is to equal or exceed the metal thickness through which the core is to pass*. If the core is rectangular, *the shortest distance across the flats is to equal or exceed the metal thickness through which the core is to pass*.

When green sand cores become impracticable, *dry sand* cores are introduced into the mold. Dry sand cores are made

FIG. 71.—Sectional view of the drag part of the mold for the clamp.

independent of the mold. They are shaped in a form called a *core-box*. The stability of dry sand cores is due to the mixture of sand used (*core sand*), which requires the core to be placed in an oven and *thoroughly dried*.

Figure 71 shows the clamp mold with the vertical *dry sand* core in place, which forms the rectangular opening through the casting. In order to show the core in place, a part of the mold has been cut away. (Sectional view shown.) *Note* how the parting of the mold has been arranged to conform to the irregularity of the cope surface of the pattern.

To receive and secure the core in its correct position in the mold, *a depression or seat is formed, as at D.* This seat is formed by the projection upon the pattern at *E*, Fig. 70, called a *core-print.*

A *core-print* is that part of a pattern which forms a *seat or depression in the sand,* which locates and secures the core within the mold.

The metal thickness of the clamp through which the core will pass is 1⅛ inches. The dimension across the flats of the core is ⅞ inch. *The distance across the flats being less than the metal thickness, a dry sand core is used.*

Stock required: 1½ × 2¼ × 7¼ inches   Body
             ¾ × 1½ × 2 inches   Core-print

ORDER OF OPERATIONS

1. Dress material to thickness—length and width of pattern, then locate the center lines.

2. Upon the surface selected for the drag face of the pattern, lay out the rectangular outline of the pad *B* and the cored hole.

To lay out the square outline of either the pad or the cored hole, scribe a circumference the diameter of which is equal to the distance across the flats; then circumscribe a square. Scribe the tangent lines with the aid of a bevel set to *45 degrees.*

The Bevel.—The bevel consists of a stock with a slotted blade that can be set and locked at any angle. A bevel is set to an angle as shown in Fig. 72.

The protractor, as illustrated in Fig. 72, is made by dividing a semicircumference into 36 equal divisions.

Bevel Protractor.—A bevel protractor as illustrated in Fig. 73 consists of an adjustable rule, held firmly at any point by a thumb nut. The rule passes through a revolving turret which is graduated in degrees from 0 to 90, both right and left, and can be accurately adjusted to show any angle.

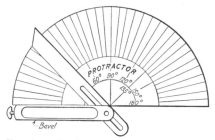

Fig. 72.—Setting a bevel to an angle.

3. Upon each edge lay out the side view of the pattern, then dress the work to this outline. *Note* the surfaces requiring *machine-finish*.

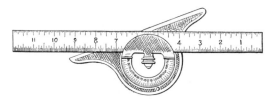

Fig. 73.—Bevel protractor.

4. Gage the thickness of the ribs *C*, then dress the pad and the ribs to shape.

The Firmer-gouge.—The firmer-gouge is used in performing this operation. It is commonly called an *outside ground gouge*, because the bevel of the cutting edge is ground on the convex face of the blade. Its action is that of digging. It is used to dress out filleted corners and surfaces that cannot be shaped with a paring-gouge. Figure 74 illustrates the manner of holding a firmer-gouge. Pressure is exerted upon the handle of the gouge with the right hand. The gouge is controlled by firmly gripping the blade with the left hand. To produce a *shearing cut,* slightly oscillate the gouge as it is moved forward. For convenience, the work is held in a hand-screw. The hand-screw is secured in the vise.

5. Make the core-print. The core-print is *sandpapered* before it is attached. Small flat surfaces like those of the core-print, are more easily and correctly sandpapered if the sandpaper is held flat upon the surface of the bench with the thumb and second finger. The work is rubbed upon the sandpaper. For the dimension *G* of the core-print, refer to *column F of the table of core-print proportions, page 70.*

Fig. 74.—Position of holding a firmer-gouge.

6. Attach the core-print.

Apply a *small amount* of glue to the core-print and *rub* the core-print upon the surface to which it is attached. Allow the glue to *set* for a few minutes, then reinforce the joint with one, 1¼-inch brad. *Bore a pilot hole for the brad.*

7. Round the corners, then finish the pattern.

Shellac the core-print portion of the pattern a *different color,* in order that it may be distinguished from the surface of the pattern which gives shape to the metal. The same *marking* is used on the surface of a pattern, to indicate the *shape* and the *location* of a core that comes just to the surface of a casting. This feature is referred to as: "*The core cuts through.*" The core which forms the hole in the clamp *cuts through.*

CORE-BOX FOR THE CLAMP PATTERN

Features presented:
  A parted core-box
  Dowel-pins
  Calculating the depth of auger-bit holes
A core-box is a form in which a core is shaped.

A parted core-box is made up of two or more parts. The core-box for the clamp is a parted core-box. The dry sand core for the clamp and the core-box in which it is formed, are illustrated in Fig. 75.

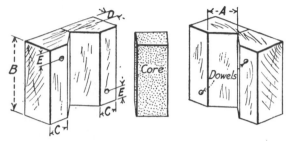

Fig. 75.—The core and core-box used in connection with the clamp pattern.

Dowel-pins.—Dowel-pins are used to keep the two halves of a parted core-box in their proper relation during the forming of the core The dowels, or dowel-pins, are inserted in one half of the box, and their pointed ends made to project, in order that they will enter holes in the opposite half. The point of a dowel should be *so shaped* as to prevent any looseness between the two parts, but yet allow their *instant release or separation*. The point proportions for wood dowels is shown in Fig. 76. Make the length A equal to the diameter of the dowel stock. Make dimension B ¼ of A, and C equal to ½ of A. *Dress* the point of a dowel-pin to shape before setting it in *place*.

Fig. 76.— W o o d dowels in place.

The size and shape of the work should determine the diameter of dowel to be used. Dowels are more *effective* if placed as *far apart* as the work will permit. The common practice of inserting *wood* dowels, as shown in Fig. 76, is to locate their position upon the parting surface. Holes are then bored through this half of the material, the two halves are then securely clamped together and the holes transferred or continued into the opposite half. *Do not bore the holes* that receive the points of the dowel, deeper than is necessary.

The depth of a hole bored with an auger-bit may be roughly calculated by counting the number of revolutions from the instant the bit begins to cut. The reason for this is that the lead screw will cause the bit to travel forward at each revolu-

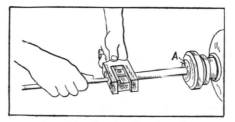

Fig. 77.—Cutting dowel stock.

tion a distance *equal to the lead of its thread.* This distance for any size auger-bit can be quickly determined by one or two trials.

Figure 77 illustrates how dowel stock may be cut with a dowel-pin cutter in the lathe, the material being revolved by one end of the stick being inserted into the chuck *A,* which is attached to a face plate. Figure 78 shows the separated parts of the cutter. *B* is a wooden handle into which is secured the

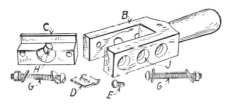

Fig. 78.—The separated parts of the dowel cutter.

Fig. 79.—Brass dowels in place.

metal part *C.* *D* is the blade. It is secured to *C* with the screw *E.* The bolts *G* secure part *C* in place in the handle *B.* The hole *H,* in part *C,* should be drilled $\frac{1}{64}$ inch larger than the diameter of the dowel. The diameter of hole *J* in the handle should be equal to the diagonal dimension of the stock.   About $\frac{1}{16}$ inch should be allowed across the flats of the stock for the cutting operation.

Dowels from $\frac{3}{16}$ to 1 inch in diameter may be purchased from any pattern supply house.

To insert brass dowels, as shown in Fig. 79, locate the position *of one of the dowels* upon the parting surface, place the head of a *small brad* at this location and press parts together.   The brad head will make an *impression in each piece* thus locating the centers of the holes to be bored. *Set* the pin and socket; then place parts together and register in a like manner the location of the next dowel.

If the method of inserting wood dowels is applied to brass dowels, the unoccupied portion of the auger-bit holes is plugged up.

A slight interference between the pins and sockets may be overcome by placing the material together and striking it a sharp blow with a mallet.

When the shape of a core-box or pattern is the same about its center line, the better practice is to *offset* the dowels so that the *misplacement* of the parts will be instantly detected. Another way to guard against this frequent error is to use two dowels of *different diameter*.

When the length of a core is 3 *inches or less*, the core cavity may be formed in a transverse direction to the grain of the wood, as shown in Fig. 75.   Only those external surfaces or dimensions of a core-box which give shape to the core are *important*.

Dimension A is the distance across the flats of the core. Dimension B is taken from the pattern.   *It is equal to the metal thickness through which the core is to pass, plus the dimension G*, Fig. 70, of the core-print.

Permanency of dimension and form of the core cavity depends upon the surrounding wood: therefore the dimensions C and D must be so proportioned as to give sufficient strength and durability, dimension E is unimportant.

Stock required: $1\frac{1}{4} \times 2 \times 7\frac{1}{4}$ inches
Dowel stock: $\frac{1}{4}$ dia. $\times 3\frac{1}{2}$ inches

ORDER OF OPERATIONS

1. Prepare the parting surfaces, then locate and set the dowels.

2. Plane one edge true and square to the parting surface.

3. Dress the width of the material to dimension *B*.

4. Locate center line, then upon both edge surfaces lay out the shape of the *core cavity*.

5. Scribe lines across the parting surface which represents the diagonal dimension of the core cavity.

6. Saw and dress core cavity to shape.

Sandpaper the core cavity with the aid of the square corner of a block. The finishing of a core-box consists of sandpapering and shellacking the *core cavity, the parting surface,* and those *exterior surfaces* which give shape to the core. The same *color shellac* is to be applied to the surfaces of the core-box that is applied to the surfaces of the pattern which represents metal. Slightly chamfering the sharp outside edges will prevent the wood splintering through usage.

Always stamp the number of a pattern or core-box in such a surface that will cause the marking to be *clearly in view.* Do not stamp the number of the pattern in the *face surface* of a core box nor in the surface of a *core cavity* where it will interfere with the removal of the box from the core.

TABLE OF CORE-PRINT PROPORTIONS

The dimensions of core-prints given in the table have been found satisfactory when applied to cores of a round or rectangular cross section, and which are set in a *horizontal* or *vertical* position in the mold. The core-prints shown in Fig. 80 are for cores set in a vertical position in the mold.

When the print is of circular cross section, it is the usual practice to attach the print to the body of the pattern with a *dowel* as shown in broken lines at *A*.

Core-prints of a rectangular cross section are attached with glue and brads. When a core-print of rectangular cross section is required to be parted from the body of the pattern, it is attached with *two dowels*.

Column C of the table is the diameter of a core if round or the shortest distance across the flats of a core if rectangular.

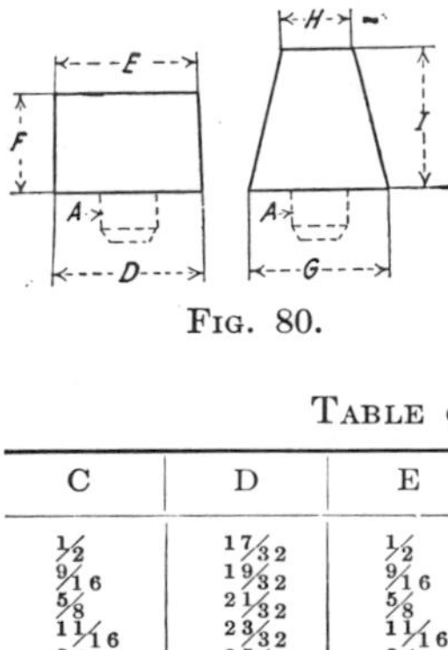

FIG. 80.

Columns D, E, and F give the dimensions for *drag core-prints*.

Columns G, H and I give the dimensions for *cope core-prints*.

Column K gives the length of core-prints for cores which are set *horizontally* in the mold.

TABLE OF CORE-PRINT PROPORTIONS

C	D	E	F	G	H	I	K
1/2	17/32	1/2	1/2	1/2	1/4	1/2	1/2
9/16	19/32	9/16	1/2	9/16	9/32	9/16	9/16
5/8	21/32	5/8	1/2	5/8	5/16	5/8	5/8
11/16	23/32	11/16	1/2	11/16	11/32	11/16	11/16
3/4	25/32	3/4	1/2	3/4	3/8	3/4	3/4
13/16	27/32	13/16	1/2	13/16	13/32	13/16	13/16
7/8	29/32	7/8	5/8	7/8	7/16	7/8	7/8
15/16	31/32	15/16	5/8	15/16	15/32	15/16	7/8
1	1 1/32	1	3/4	1	1/2	1	7/8
1 1/16	1 3/32	1 1/16	3/4	1 1/16	17/32	1 1/16	7/8
1 1/8	1 5/32	1 1/8	3/4	1 1/8	9/16	1 1/8	7/8
1 3/16	1 7/32	1 3/16	3/4	1 3/16	19/32	1 3/16	7/8
1 1/4	1 9/32	1 1/4	7/8	1 1/4	5/8	1 1/4	7/8
1 5/16	1 11/32	1 5/16	7/8	1 5/16	21/32	1 5/16	1
1 3/8	1 13/32	1 3/8	7/8	1 3/8	11/16	1 3/8	1
1 7/16	1 15/32	1 7/16	7/8	1 7/16	23/32	1 7/16	1
1 1/2	1 17/32	1 1/2	1	1 1/2	3/4	1 1/2	1
1 9/16	1 19/32	1 9/16	1	1 9/16	13/16	1 1/2	1
1 5/8	1 21/32	1 5/8	1	1 5/8	7/8	1 1/2	1
1 11/16	1 23/32	1 11/16	1	1 11/16	15/16	1 1/2	1
1 3/4	1 25/32	1 3/4	1	1 3/4	1	1 1/2	1
1 13/16	1 27/32	1 13/16	1	1 13/16	1 1/16	1 1/2	1 1/8
1 7/8	1 29/32	1 7/8	1	1 7/8	1 1/8	1 1/2	1 1/8
1 15/16	1 31/32	1 15/16	1	1 15/16	1 3/16	1 1/2	1 1/8
2	2 1/32	2	1	2	1 1/4	1 1/2	1 1/8
2 1/4	2 9/32	2 1/4	1	2 1/4	1 1/2	1 1/2	1 1/8
2 1/2	2 17/32	2 1/2	1	2 1/2	1 3/4	1 1/2	1 1/8
3	3 1/32	3	1	3	2	1 1/2	1 1/8

QUESTIONS

1. From what source is glue obtained?

2. Describe how glue is prepared for use.

3. Describe the arrangement of a kettle for heating glue.

4. What are the essentials of a good glue joint?

5. What is understood by sizing as applied to a glue joint?

6. How is the size of wire brads specified?

7. What is understood by toeing a brad?

8. How should a brad be driven in end grain wood to obtain the greatest withdrawal resistance?

9. When two or more brads are used in the same locality, how should they be placed?

10. How may a brad be driven through a fragile piece of material without danger of splitting it?

11. What is a nail-set?

12. For what purpose is the trimmer used?

13. Why are the sharp inside corners of patterns filleted?

14. What kind of fillet material is recognized as giving the best result?

15. What is the procedure followed in affixing leather fillet?

16. Describe an arrangement for making wax fillet.

17. What is a dry sand core?

18. What rule may be applied to determine between the use of a green sand and a dry sand core?

19. What is a core-box?

20. What is a core-print?

21. Describe the tool known as the bevel.

22. What is a protractor?

23. How does a firmer-gouge differ from a paring-gouge?

24. For what nature of work is the firmer-gouge principally used?

25. How is a slicing cut produced with a firmer-gouge?

26. Why is the core-print portion of a pattern shellacked a different color than the surface of the pattern which gives shape to the metal?

27. What is to be understood by the expression, "the core cuts through?" How is it indicated on the pattern?

28. What is a parted core-box?

29. What is the purpose of dowel-pins?

30. Describe the mode of procedure followed in setting a brass dowel-pin.

PATTERN 6

LINK

Features presented:
  Parted patterns
  Contraction for steel
Figure 81 is the drawing of a cast steel link.

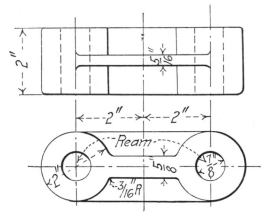

FIG. 81.

Patterns are nothing more nor less than tools to be used by the molder in forming a mold; *therefore, every effort should be made in their arrangement and construction to further their purpose.*

To accomplish this end, a great number of objects require special features to be embodied in the pattern's construction. A common feature is that of *parting the pattern,* or making the pattern in *two or more parts.* When made in two parts, the parts take their name from the section of the flask in which they are molded, as the *cope or drag part* of the pattern.

78

Figure 82A illustrates the parting of a mold for a *parted* link pattern, and Fig. 82B, the parting for a *solid* link pattern. No better example is needed to show the advantage of the parted pattern feature. Compare the parting of the mold, made by the *parted* pattern, with the parting required to be made for the *solid* pattern.

Fig. 82A.—The parting surface of a mold made by a parted link pattern.

Fig. 82B.—The parting surface of a mold required to be made for a solid link pattern.

In the case of the parted pattern, the mold-board produces *a plane parting*, while in the case of the solid pattern, it is necessary to make an *irregular parting* about the pattern, as shown. This extra work adds to the cost of production. An irregular parting adds to the difficulties of lifting off the cope, and very frequently results in the *defacement* of the mold. Further advantage of a *parted pattern* lies in the fact that the *cope half* of the pattern is lifted off with the *cope;* this part of the pattern is then drawn in the usual way.

The cast steel link is composed of two *bosses*. The bosses are connected by a member called the *web*. A *rib* upon each face of the web further strengthens the casting. The ⅞-inch holes through the bosses must be reamed. The operation of drilling precedes that of reaming. *The information given with Pattern 3, page 55, regarding drilled holes, applies also to reamed holes.*

Figure 83 shows the two halves of the pattern in different stages of completion; it also gives the names of the members. The shape of the link suggests that its pattern be *parted* through the center of the *web* or axis of bosses, as shown.

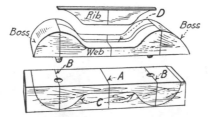

FIG. 83.—The drag and cope part of the link pattern at different stages of completion.

Refer to the instruction on contraction of metal, given with Pattern 1, page 42.

Stock required: 1 ⅛ × 2¼ × 13 inches   Body
⁷⁄₁₆ × ⅞ × 8¼ inches   Ribs

ORDER OF OPERATIONS

1. Prepare the parting. *Make a good joint between the two parts.*

2. Place the dowel-pins in about the position shown. *Refer to the information on dowel-pins, page 72.*

If the requirements or the form of casting require that the pattern be parted; the dowel pins are to be set in the *cope part of the pattern.* If set in the drag part of the pattern, they will interfere with the *placing* of the pattern upon the mold-board.

3. Dress the material to the required width of pattern.

4. Scribe upon the parting of the drag half, the center lines *A* and *B*, then place the parts together and transfer these lines to the cope half of the pattern.

5. Scribe upon each edge surface of the material the circumferences of the bosses.

6. From the parting, gage the half thickness of the web,

then scribe the fillet *C*, which connects the surface of the web with that of the bosses. Scribe lines across the parting surfaces to represent the over-all length of the pattern.

Attention is called to the fillets *C*. These fillets are dressed out during the shaping of the pattern. *There would be no advantage in making the line of intersection between the surface of the web and that of the boss, a sharp corner, then affixing a leather fillet.*

7. Saw and dress the work to outline, then finish this surface with sandpaper. Gage lines as indicated by *D*, which represent the location of the *ribs*. Figure 83 shows the cope half of the pattern at this stage of completion, and ready to receive the rib.

8. Prepare the rib material. *Do not plane to width.* To obtain the *shape* of the joint between the bosses and the rib, hold the rib material against the face of the bosses and in its correct relation to the surface of the web, and then trace the outline of the bosses upon it.

9. With the gouge, pare the concave joint surface of the ribs to shape.

10. *Draft* the sides of the ribs and then glue in place. *Do not brad.*

11. Allow the glue to set for a few minutes, then plane the edge of the ribs tangent to the bosses. Further secure each rib with two 1-inch brads. Drive the brads through the ribs and into the bosses at an angle. Place the brads about ¾ inch from the ends of the ribs.

12. Draft the face of the bosses.

13. Affix the fillets, *⅛-inch fillet.*

14. Break the corners (remove the sharp corners) of the pattern with sandpaper. *This is not to apply to the corners of the parting surface.*

15. Finish the pattern. The *parting surfaces* of a pattern are given the same *shellac finish* as the surfaces which give shape to the mold.

6

PATTERN 7

GUIDE

Features presented:
Contraction of brass
Finish-allowance for brass
Securing a vertical dry sand core at both ends
Cope core-prints
Avoiding the exposure of end grain wood
Application of dowel-pins
Hand-screws

Figure 84 is the drawing of a brass guide.

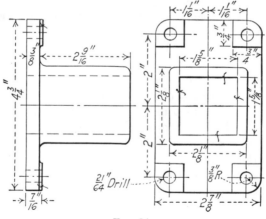

FIG. 84.

If the *metal thickness* through which a vertical dry sand core is to pass equals *two or more times* the shortest distance across the flats if the core is rectangular, or the diameter of the core if it is round, it is a safe practice to secure the core at *both ends*.

82

The metal thickness through which the core for the guide passes equals twice the distance across the *flats of the core*. Therefore the core will be secured at *both ends* as illustrated by a sectional view of the mold, Fig. 85. It is done by forming in the parting of the cope a *tapered impression* as indicated by *A*, directly above the core print impression *B* in the drag. The *tapered walls* of the depression *A* correspond to the *taper*

Fig. 85.—Sectional view of the drag part of the mold for the guide.

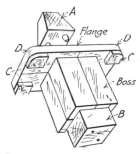

Fig. 86.—The pattern for the guide.

at the top end of the core, and is the means of correctly registering the core by the placing on of the cope.

The pattern for the guide is shown in Fig. 86. It is made up of a *flange*, a rectangular *boss*, and the core prints *A* and *B*. Four *pads* are attached to the flange as at *C*.

The *cope core print A* is shown opposite the position it occupies upon the top surface of the flange. Making the *cope print* loose permits the print to *lift off with the cope*. It also allows the *face of the flange to lie flat* upon the mold board.

Finish marks show that machine-finish is required on the internal surfaces of the boss. A frequent mistake made when shaping the core prints is the failure to allow the finish allowance upon the four walls. One *sixteenth of an inch finish allowance* will be allowed on the surfaces of *brass castings*.

Refer to the instruction on contraction of metal given with Pattern 1, page 42.

Hand-screws.—When the material at hand is not of sufficient thickness, two or more pieces of material are *glued together.* To hold the wood together while the glue is drying, *hand-screws*, as shown in Fig. 87, are used.

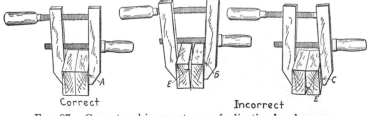

Correct   Incorrect

FIG. 87.—Correct and incorrect way of adjusting hand-screws.

The hand-screw consists of *two jaws* and *two screws.* The contacting surfaces of jaws should always bear *evenly* against the material as indicated by *A,* thereby causing the joint surfaces of the material to be forced together. The letters *B* and *C* show how the failure to adjust the jaws correctly, results in a poor or open joint, as indicated by *E.* The pressure is put upon the jaws by the end screw. The middle screw which is used for adjusting, simply serves as a fulcrum for the jaws.

Never apply glue to the material before the hand-screws have been *adjusted* to suit the work and are ready for *instant use.* To make a slight change in the spread of the jaws, loosen the end screw and adjust the middle screw as the case may require. To open or close a hand-screw, grip the handle of the middle screw in the left hand and the handle of the end screw in the right hand. To open the jaws, revolve the hand-screw *over toward you,* and to close the jaws, revolve it *over from you.*

Stock required: 2⅜ × 2⅜ × 3 inches   Boss
                ½ × 3⅛ × 5¼ inches   Flange
                1¾ × 1¾ × 4 inches   Core-prints
                ¼ × 1   × 4 inches   Pads

ORDER OF OPERATIONS

1. Dress the material for the flange to the required thickness, width and length, then locate the center lines.

2. Dress the material for the boss to the required thickness, width and length, then locate the center lines.

The grain of wood in the boss is to lie in the direction of the length of the boss. End grain wood *absorbs* moisture more *freely* than length grain. For this reason, whenever the shape of the pattern permits, the *exposure* of end grain wood should be avoided.

Accuracy of construction can be attained in no better way than to assemble the parts of a pattern by the *exact agreement of their center lines.*

3. Locate the boss upon the flange and attach with glue and brads. *Refer to the instruction on the selection of brads and the application of glue to end grain wood given with Pattern 4 page 61.*

4. Dress the material for the core-prints to the required thickness, width and length and locate the center lines. *Do not taper* the edge surfaces of the cope print. *Refer to the table of core-print proportions, page 76.*

5. Locate and bore holes through the cope print for the two dowel-pins. The dowels are to be of different diameters, ($3/16$ and $1/4$ inch). The use of dowels of different diameters is to prevent the *print from being placed in any other position than that intended.*

6. Locate the cope print in its correct position upon the flange Fig. 86 and attach temporarily with brads, then bore the holes in the flange for dowels.

7. Detach the print and insert the dowels.

8. Upon the top surface of the print, *gage* the amount the sides are to be *tapered*, then dress to shape.

9. Dress to shape and sandpaper the drag print, then attach it with glue and brads.

10. The strip of material from which the four *pads* are made, is dressed to the required thickness and width of the

pads. It is then cut up into the required lengths and attached.

Upon the surfaces of the *pads* scribe arcs representing the outline of the rounded corners of the flange as at *D*, and dress the corners to shape.

11. Finish the pattern. One-eighth-inch fillet will be used. The surface covered by a loose core-print is to have the same color as the print. *Refer to the instructions on shellacking core-prints given with Pattern 5, page 71.*

CORE-BOX FOR THE GUIDE PATTERN

Features presented:

    Making a dry sand core in halves

    Core-box for a core made in halves

    Toeing a nail

Application of draft to the surface of core cavities.

Dry sand cores are sometimes made in halves and *pasted together after having been dried.* This is often the practice when a small number of cores is required. The shape of a core will sometimes necessitate this feature. Making the core in halves saves material and time when constructing the core-box, and the plane joint surface of the half cores permits them to lie *flat* upon the *core plate* while being dried.

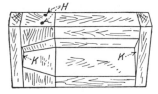

Figure 88 illustrates the core-box for the guide and the one half core formed within it. Two half cores

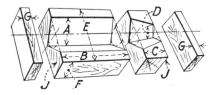

FIG. 88.—One half of the core for the guide and the core-box in which it is formed.

FIG. 89.—The parts of the core-box for guide dressed to shape and ready to be attached together.

are formed in the box, the cores are then dried, and subsequently pasted together.

The surface of a core cavity which *lies parallel* to the direction the core box is removed from the core, is to be drafted. The surfaces K, of the core cavity lie in this direction and therefore are to be given draft. Draft is provided upon these surfaces by *slightly slanting* toward the bottom of the core cavity the surfaces J, Fig. 89.

The separated pieces of material which make up the box are shown in Fig. 89. Dimensions are indicated by letters. *A* is the distance across the flats of the core. *B* is equal to the metal thickness through which the core is to pass, *plus the length* of the drag core-print. *C* and *D* are taken from the cope core-print. *E, F* and *G* are unimportant dimensions.

Stock required: $1\frac{5}{8} \times 3\frac{3}{8} \times 4\frac{3}{8}$ inches

$1\frac{5}{8} \times 1\frac{5}{8} \times 3\frac{1}{2}$ inches

$\frac{5}{6} \times 1\frac{5}{8} \times 7$ inches

ORDER OF OPERATIONS

1. True up one face and one edge of the material which is to contain the triangular core cavity, then dress the material to length *B*.

2. Locate a line along the center of the width and across each end.

3. Upon the end surfaces scribe semicircumferences as shown in broken lines, whose diameters are equal to the distance across the *flats* of the core.

4. At 45 degrees to the face of the material, scribe lines tangent to the semicircumferences. Scribe lines at such a distance apart as is represented by the diagonal dimension of the core cavity.

5. Dress the core cavity to shape.

6. Dress to dimension *C* the material for the core-print portion of the box, and scribe center line.

7. Repeat operations 3 and 4, using for the layout on one surface of the material a semicircumference whose diameter is equal to the distance across the *flats* of the top of the cope core-print.

8. Sandpaper the core cavity with the aid of the *square corner* of a block.

9. Attach the parts with glue and brads. Drive the brads at an *inclination* to the joint as at *H*, Fig. 88; this is called *toeing a nail.* Provide the draft upon the surfaces *K* and attach the end pieces.

10. Dress the edge surfaces and chamfer the corners. *Refer ot the instructions on finishing core-boxes given with Pattern 5, page 75.*

A pattern in the hands of a molder is a tool for producing castings—therefore, make patterns as effective as possible.

PATTERN 8

BRACKET

Features presented:
  Pattern construction
  The rabbet-joint
  Disc-sanding
Figure 90 is the drawing of a cast iron bracket. The casting is made up of a *web, a flange, a boss and a rib.*

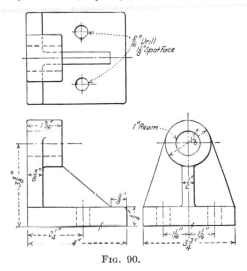

FIG. 90.

The drawing specifies that surfaces about the bolt-holes, at the back of the flange, are to be *spot-faced.* Spot-facing is the operation of truing up a circular bearing surface. *It does not affect the pattern.* The hole through the boss is to be reamed. *Refer to the instruction on reamed holes given with Pattern 6, page 79.*

89

Figure 91 shows the pattern in course of making; the flange, the web and the boss have been attached. The chief factor in pattern construction is to arrange the material in such a way

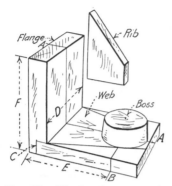

FIG. 91.—The bracket pattern in process of making.

as to *minimize distortion*, and to *preserve*, as far as possible, accuracy of *dimension and form*. The pattern for the bracket is a good lesson in pattern construction.

To obtain greater rigidity between two pieces of material that meet at an angle, as the web and the flange, *the rabbet-joint is used*. It consists of forming in the flange a rabbet, as at C, into which the web is secured. When two different thicknesses of material are secured together with a *rabbet-joint*, the rabbet is usually cut in the material of the *greater* thickness.

Material required: ¾ × 4   × 4½ inches   Web
              1 × 4   × 4½ inches   Flange
              ⅝ × 2⅛ × 4¼ inches   Rib
              ⅞ × 2¼ × 2¼ inches   Boss

ORDER OF OPERATIONS

1. Dress to thickness the material for the flange and the web and make the rabbet.

2. Draft the *inside surface* of the flange and attach the parts together. Drive the brads through the web into the flange material. *Test the work with the square.*

3. Dress the material to the width D of the flange.

4. Gage the center line A along the middle of the width of the material. Lay off the distance E and scribe the center line B about the material.

5. Lay off and dress the flange to the dimension represented by *F*.

6. Make the boss. The boss may be turned, or it may be sawed, and then *sanded to shape.*

The Disc-sander.—The disc-sander as shown in Fig. 92 is used in sanding to shape flat and convexed surfaces. The

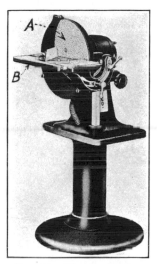

Fig. 92.—The disc-sander.

sandpaper is affixed to the face *A* of a metal disc. The table *B* is adjustable. It may be set at varying angles to the face *A* of the disc. The material for an object that is to be sanded to shape is prepared in the same way as for chisel paring, with this exception: *The layout is made upon one face of the material only.*

The *grain* of the wood in the boss when attached should lie in the *same direction as the grain* of the wood in the web.

When a surface of a pattern is formed by two or more thicknesses of material glued together, the grain of the wood should *lie in the same direction.* End grain wood and cross grain wood are not affected the same by moisture. Therefore, a surface made up of end and cross grain wood will likely become uneven.

7. Attach the boss. To locate the boss upon the web, scribe a circumference which is the diameter of the boss.

8. From the corner edges of the flange, scribe lines tangent to the boss as shown, and saw the web to shape. The shape of the web may be planed and pared to shape, or it may be *sanded to shape.*

9. Prepare the rib material; fit it into place; then dress the edge to the required angle. Attach the rib.

10. Round the corners. *All corners of patterns are to be rounded to approximately $\frac{1}{16}$-inch radius,* unless otherwise instructed. *Do not round the corners of a surface which is to be finished.*

11. Affix the fillets, then finish the pattern.

Reminders

Don't leave the gluing up of stock until the material is needed.

Don't get out the material for a pattern piecemeal; but get out the complete list at one time

Don't expend unnecessary time in giving patterns a high polish; they are not used as ornaments, but are used in the production of castings.

Don't stand around when waiting for a job, there are always tools to be sharpened.

PATTERN 9

PEDESTAL

Features presented:
Contraction for aluminum
Parting pattern
Parted core-prints
Supporting at both ends a core set horizontally in a mold
Cope clearance at the ends of cores set horizontally.
Figure 93 is the drawing of an aluminum pedestal.

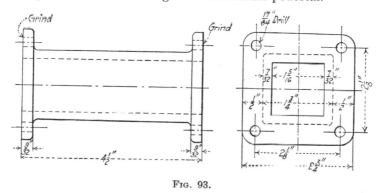

FIG. 93.

The casting consists of two flanges connected by a body, or shell, of a rectangular cross section. The drawing specifies that the faces of the flanges are to be ground.

Grind, when applied to a casting, means that a surface is to be trued up by the use of an abrasive wheel or disc. Unless the drawing states that an amount of stock is to be allowed for this operation, no attention is given to it by the pattern-maker.

For small castings of a rectangular cross section, it is usually good practice to part the pattern *diagonally*. This arrange-

93

ment facilitates the *drawing* of the pattern, as well as the *setting* of the core into the mold.

Figure 94 illustrates the drag part of the mold with the core in place. The core is located and held in place by the seats

Fig. 94.—Drag part of the mold for the pedestal.

A, formed by the core-prints extending out from the ends of the pattern.

The ends of the cope half of the prints are made to *overhang* the drag half, as shown in Fig. 95. This is to give *clearance*

Fig. 95.—A portion of the pedestal pattern illustrating how provision (overhang) is made on the end of core-print to provide cope clearance.

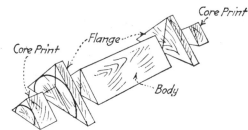

Fig. 96.—Members of the drag part of the pedestal pattern shaped and ready to be attached together.

and prevent the cope from touching the end surfaces of the core during the *closing of the mold*. For small cores, this overhang is to be $\frac{1}{16}$ inch. *No attention* is given this *overhang* feature when making the core-box, as the length of the core is made to suit the drag half of the pattern.

The parts which go to make up the drag half of the pattern are shown in Fig. 96.

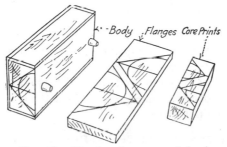

Fig. 97.—Members in process of shaping.

The shape of the parts for one half of the pattern is shown laid out upon the material, Fig. 97.

Refer to the instruction on contraction of metal given with Pattern 1, page 42.

Stock required: 1⅜ × 2¾ × 8¾ inches   Body
               ⅜ × 2⅜ × 11 inches   Flanges
               1⅛ × 1⅜ × 6½ inches   Core-prints

ORDER OF OPERATIONS

1. Select the material for the body; prepare the parting, then set the dowels, Fig. 97.

2. Place the parts together and dress the work to length.

3. Lay out the shape of the body upon the ends, then dress to its rectangular cross section.

4. Prepare the material for the flanges and the core-prints. A saving of material will result if the shape of these members is laid out upon the wood as shown, Fig. 97.

Note.—Allow for the *overhang* in preparing the material for the prints on the cope half of the pattern.

For the length of the core-prints, refer to the table of core-print proportions, page 76.

The parts of the pattern may be accurately shaped, but unless they are *correctly assembled*, the pattern is worthless.

5. Assemble the drag part of the pattern first. *Hold* the parting surfaces of the flanges firmly down upon a flat surface when gluing them to the body. *Rub* the joint surfaces together; *do not* use hand-screws. Allow the glue to set about 10 minutes, then reinforce the joints with brads.

6. Attach the core-prints in the same manner as the flanges.

7. *Assemble the cope half* of the pattern upon the *drag half*. A piece of paper placed upon the parting of the drag will prevent any surplus glue from affixing the cope to the drag.

8. Finish the pattern.

CORE-FRAME FOR THE PEDESTAL PATTERN

Features presented:

Core-frame construction

Drag clearance at the ends of the core set horizontally

The dado-joint

The router

The saw-bench

Cores of rectangular shape are usually formed in a core-box or frame, as shown in Fig. 98. The inside dimensions of

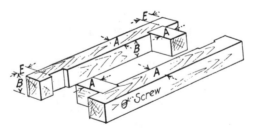

Fig. 98.—Core-frame used in connection with the pedestal pattern.

the frame represent the required dimensions of the core. With the exception of the depth B, the outside dimensions of the frame are unimportant. The material from which a core-frame is made should be of sufficient, *thickness A* to withstand *without distortion* the ramming in of the sand. For large frames, the thickness A will vary somewhat with the depth B, but for small sized frames as herewith discussed, ⅛ *inch* will be strong enough.

When the cross section of the core which is supported at both ends, is the same throughout its length, make the *length* of the core ¹⁄₁₆ *of an inch less* than the distance between the end surfaces of the drag prints. This amount of *clearance* permits the core to enter the print depressions without *end interference*.

To sustain permanency of form, the ends and side pieces of the frame are secured together with the dado-joint. The width of the surface is first sawed to the required depth; the waste is then removed with a chisel, and the surface finished with the router.

The Router.—The router is used for smoothing the face of depressed surfaces. Figure 99 illustrates how a router is used

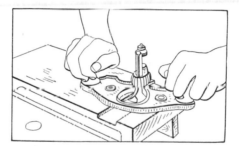

Fig. 99.—Finishing the depressed surface of a dado with a router.

in smoothing the face of the depressed surface of a *dado*. *Do not attempt to take a heavy cut with a router.*

Stock required: 1 piece 1 × 3⅛ × 12½ inches

ORDER OF OPERATIONS

Figure 100 illustrates how the ends and side pieces of the frame are made from one piece of material.

1. Prepare the material; dress the ends, then plane to a parallel width. Allow about ¼ inch for the separation of the material along the middle of its width.

7

2. From one end of the material lay off the length dimensions of the side pieces; make dimension *E* of the side pieces equal to the thickness *A*.

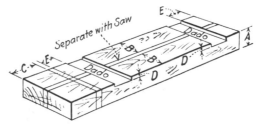

FIG. 100.—The material for the core-frame in process of shaping.

3. Layout and dress the dadoes to shape. The dimension *D* of the dadoes will be ⅛ inch.

4. From the opposite end of the material lay off the length *C* of the end pieces. The length *C* of the end pieces is equal to the distance *across the flats* of the core, plus two times *D*.

FIG. 101.—Saw bench.

5. Dress end and side pieces to length, then separate parts and dress to dimension *B*.

Each end piece is attached to a side piece with a screw placed at the point shown, Fig. 98.

6. Chamfer the outside corners, $\frac{1}{16}$ inch chamfer. The *diagonal corners* of the frame are unattached, as shown; *this permits the frame to be easily removed from the core.*

The Saw-bench.—The universal saw-bench as illustrated in Fig. 101 is a very important machine used in pattern work for ripping, cross-cut sawing and grooving.

Rabbet and *dado-joints* are usually made upon the saw-bench.

The universal saw-bench is provided with both rip and cross-cut-saws, either of which may be brought into action by turning a hand wheel.

The table may be tilted at any angle from zero to 45 degrees.

QUESTIONS

1. How may the depth of a hole bored with an auger-bit be roughly calculated?

2. Describe an arrangement for making wood dowel-pin stock.

3. Describe a method followed in inserting brass dowels.

4. What is a parted pattern?

5. What advantage is gained by parting the link pattern?

6. Name the members composing the link casting.

7. What is the contraction allowance for steel castings?

8. How should the parting surface of a parted pattern be finished?

9. What rule may be applied to determine the use of a cope core-print?

10. Why is the cope core-print of the guide pattern tapered?

11. What is the object in making the cope-print of the guide pattern loose or parting it from the flange?

12. What contraction allowance is made for brass?

13. What is the usual finish allowance provided upon the surface of brass castings?

14. Explain how the jaws of a hand-screw are adjusted to suit a piece of work.

15. Why are dowel-pins of different diameters used to attach the cope core-print of the guide pattern?

16. Why is it preferable to make a core-box for one half of the core for the guide casting?

17. When is the rabbet-joint used in pattern construction?

18. For what purpose is the disc-sander used?

19. What is the term grind understood to mean when applied to the surface of a casting?

20. What is the advantage gained in parting the pedestal pattern diagonally?

21. What is understood by the term overhang as applied to a core print?

22. What is the name of the joint commonly used to secure together the sides and end pieces of core-frames?

23. For what purpose is the router used?

24. What is the contraction allowance for aluminum?

25. Why are the diagonal corners of a core-frame unattached?

26. What is a saw-bench?

Reminders

Don't use machine tools or appliances until proper instruction has been given as to their use and care.

Don't wear loose clothing when operating machinery. The sleeves of clothing should always be rolled up.

Don't touch a broken band-saw blade until the lower wheel of the saw has stopped revolving.

Don't leave the jointer set with a heavy cut, always adjust the table.

Don't discard material which has protruding nail points, it is dangerous.

Acquire habits of caution for your own protection and for that of your shop mate.

PATTERN 10

PAWL

Features presented:
Counter-sawing
Spoke-shave
Figure 102 is the drawing of a cast steel pawl.

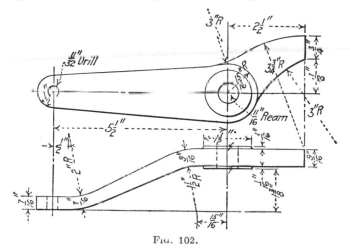

Fig. 102.

Pattern members similar in form to the plate portion of the pawl pattern, are usually shaped by what is termed *counter-sawing*. It is the method of sawing to shape the outline which represents two views of a pattern member from a piece of material of a rectangular cross section. This method of shaping a member will cause an excess amount of waste; however, *the time saved* will more than compensate for the loss of material.

Stock required: $2\frac{1}{4} \times 3\frac{1}{2} \times 9\frac{1}{2}$ inches   Plate
$\frac{3}{8} \times 1\frac{3}{4} \times 4$ inches   Bosses

101

ORDER OF OPERATIONS

1. Dress the material to the required dimension C of the pattern.   Make width D of the material about $3\frac{1}{4}$ inches.

2. Dress one end, and from this surface lay off and scribe the center lines E and F.   Gage the center line G about $1\frac{1}{4}$ inches from one edge of the material.

3. Upon one face of the material, lay out the *top view* of the plate.   Upon one edge of the material, lay out the *front view* of the plate.

4. Saw the plate to the outline of its *front view* Fig. 102. Figure 103 shows the work at the completion of this operation.

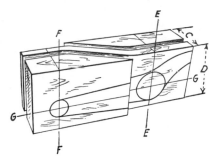

Fig. 103.—The work at the completion of the first sawing operation.

5. Rescribe upon both faces of the plate the portion of the center lines destroyed by the sawing operation, then brad the parts together.

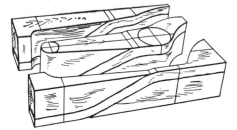

Fig. 104.—The work at the completion of the second sawing operation.

6. Saw the plate to the outline of its *top view*.   Illustration Figure 104 shows the work at the completion of this operation.

7. Finish the surfaces of the plate and attach the bosses.

Figure 105 shows how a *spoke-shave* is used to dress the surfaces of the plate. For convenience, the plate is held in a hand-screw. The hand-screw is secured in a vise.

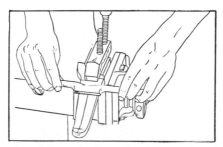

FIG. 105.—Dressing with a spoke-shave the plate member of the pawl pattern.

The Spoke-shave.—The spoke-shave works on the same principle as a plane. The guiding surface being very short makes it adaptable to surfaces of a curved nature. The control of the spoke-shave depends upon a *sensitive touch*. If lightly gripped, it may be easily guided over the surface of the work.

The blade of a spoke-shave is secured into the handle with two binding posts.

The blade is ground upon a narrow face abrasive wheel. It is best whetted on the edge surface of a small oil-stone, as shown, Fig. 106. By securing the stone in a block and then holding the block in the vise as shown, the binding posts of the blade are clear of any interference.

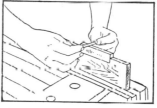

FIG. 106.—Whetting a spoke-shave blade.

It is very important that the face side of the blade be preserved in perfect condition. Do all the *grinding and whetting* on the beveled side. Never touch the face except to remove the wire-edge, and then be careful to hold the face of the blade *flat upon the stone.*

PATTERN 11

SUPPORT

Features presented:
Shaping patterns

Figure 107 is the drawing of a cast iron support. The casting is composed of a cylindrical shaped body, a pad, and a clamping-lug.

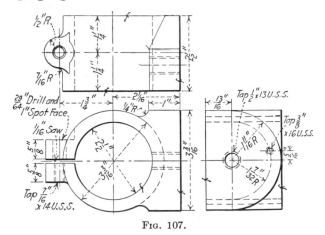

FIG. 107.

The drawing shows a *saw cut* through the center of the thickness of the lug. The note, "$\frac{1}{16}$-inch saw," indicates the thickness of the slitting saw or *cutter* to be used. *It does not affect the pattern.*

A tapped hole is required in one half the thickness of the lug. Tapping is the operation of *threading a hole*. The operation of drilling precedes that of tapping. The information previously given regarding drilled holes, *applies also to tapped holes.*

104

The 2½-inch hole through the casting requires finish. Unless otherwise instructed, *finished holes* in iron castings of 1¼-inch diameter or less, *will be drilled*. Finished holes greater than 1¼-inch diameter will be *cored ¼ inch less in diameter than the finished size*.

The shape in a great number of small castings makes it more practicable to dress the members of the pattern out of

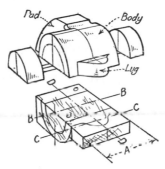

Fig. 108.—The drag and cope part of the support pattern at different stages of completion.

solid wood. The pattern for the table support is a good lesson of this kind. Figure 108 shows the drag and the cope half of the pattern at different stages in the making.

Stock required: 1¾ × 3 × 10 inches   Body
             1¼ × 2½ × 10½ inches   Core-print

ORDER OF OPERATIONS

1. Prepare the parting and set the dowels.

2. Reduce the material to the width *A* of the pattern, then dress the end surface which is to be the face of the pad.

3. Upon the parting of the drag half of the pattern, scribe the center lines *B*, *C* and *D*.

4. Transfer the center lines to the cope half, then lay out the side views of the pattern.

5. Dress the work to this shape. The drag half of the pattern is shown at this *stage of completion*.

6. Lay out the shape of the *lug* upon the parting, and also upon the faces of the lug.

7. Dress the lug to shape. The cope half of the pattern is shown at this *stage of completion*.

8. Upon the end surface of the material locate the center of the circular shape of the *pad*, then scribe this outline.

9. Dress to shape the lateral surface of the pad, and the adjacent surface of the body of the pattern.

The core-prints are sawed, then pared or sanded to shape. *Refer to the instruction on providing clearance at the end of cores, given with Pattern 9, pages 94 and 97.*

CORE-BOX FOR THE SUPPORT PATTERN

Features presented:
    Shaping semicircular core-cavities
    Arranging the material for core-boxes
    Roughing out the core cavity upon circular saw
    The core-box plane
    The rabbet-plane
    Testing the accuracy of a semicircular core-cavity
    Stock required: 1¾ × 4 × 11 inches

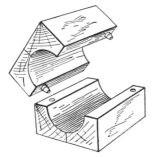

FIG. 109.—Core-box used in connection with the support pattern.

FIG. 110.—The waste material removed by a series of saw-cuts.

When cylindrical cores, as required for the table support, are wanted in number, a core-box as illustrated in Fig. 109, is made.

Material of ample length to make both halves of the box is laid out and dressed to shape; it is then sawed and dressed to the required lengths and doweled together as shown.

Semicircular core-boxes of 3½ inches or less in diameter are usually worked out of solid material. The greater part of the waste is removed from the core cavity by a *series*

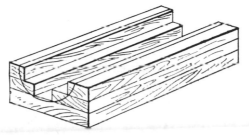

Fig. 111.—Method of stepping up the material for semicircular core-boxes.

of saw cuts as shown in Fig. 110. To save material, core-boxes between 3½ inches and 6 inches in diameter are stepped up as shown in Fig. 111.

The surface of the concavity is then carried to completion with a bent handle gouge, or a core-box plane.

When the surface is to be finished with the *gouge*, the saw cuts should be made to the *line*, then used as a guide in completing the surface.

When the cavity is to be shaped with a *core-box plane*, as shown in Fig. 112, allow ½ inch to remain as at *D*, to be removed with this tool.

The Core-box Plane.—The core-box plane is constructed on the principle of a square. The sides are at an angle of 90 degrees to each other.

The core-box plane is not confined to straight semicircular cavities as

Fig. 112.—S h a p i n g a semicircular core cavity with a core-box plane.

shown. It is also used in dressing out cavities of *tapered form*. In dressing out a cavity of this shape a greater amount of material *must be removed* toward the large diameter of the cavity, otherwise the faces of the plane will not bear evenly upon the edges of the cavity throughout the length of the work.

To start and guide a core-box plane throughout the length of the first cut, a *rabbet* of $\frac{1}{32}$-inch depth is made as at *E* Fig. 112. The rabbet may be made upon the saw bench or with a *rabbet-plane* as shown in Fig. 113. To guide the rabbet-plane, a strip is bradded along the line representing the edge of the core cavity.

The Rabbet-plane.—The rabbet-plane is used for planing rabbets and dadoes. The bit extends to the full width of the

FIG. 113.—The rabbet-plane.

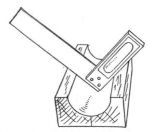

FIG. 114.—Testing with a try-square a semicircular core cavity.

face of the plane. This feature makes its application possible into corners up against perpendicular surfaces which are inaccessible to other planes. The size of a rabbet-plane is specified by the width of the face in inches.

The accuracy of a semicircular core cavity may be *tested with a square*, as shown, in Fig. 114. If the two edges of the square rest upon the edges of the core cavity as shown, the corners of the square should just touch the *concave surface at all points*. It is upon this principle that the core-box plane is constructed.

A PATTERN LAYOUT

A pattern layout is a *full-sized drawing* of one or more views of the required casting, to which *are added the pattern features.* This layout is to show the arrangement of the pattern in its construction. The location of drilled holes and other features which are purely machine-shop operations and to which the pattern-maker gives no consideration, are eliminated from the layout.

A layout of a pattern, being made in *full size*, brings into view certain features of construction that would be obscure on small scale drawing. *A layout is used as a direct reference in getting out the material and in dimensioning the work.*

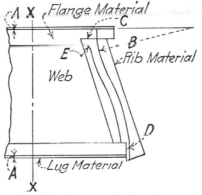

Fig. 115.—The layout of the lathe leg pattern.

A layout should be accurately made according to the contraction rule. The surfaces of the casting requiring machine-finish should be noted, and the amount of finish allowance shown on the layout. The pattern-maker works in wood; likewise his layout is made upon wood (layout board). The points which have been covered in the information pertaining to the laying out of lines on patterns, are to be applied to the layout board.

Do not use a pencil to make a layout, but when the layout is completed, the scribed lines may be further defined with a medium-hard, chisel-pointed pencil. To keep the layout clean, a single coat of shellac should be applied.

Mistakes are less apt to occur, if the layout is made to the given dimensions, (*contraction allowed*), *and the pattern features and allowances then added.*

Lay out only those views or portions of a pattern which will materially assist in the pattern's construction. Figure 115 is the layout of Pattern **12.** It is a pattern for the legs of a small bench-lathe. As the shape of the pattern is symmetrical with respect to the center line *XX*, a layout of one half of the pattern is all that is necessary.

The layout in this case is needed to determine the *thickness* of the material for the ribs, the *angle* at which it is joined to the flange material, the arrangement of the *rabbet-joints* between the flange and the ribs, and the *joints* between the lugs and ribs. To obtain the maximum strength of the ribs through the elimination of short grain wood, the placement of the material causes the shape of the ribs to lie in the direction of the grain of wood, as shown. The *finish allowance* is indicated at *A.*

Reminders

Don't make an unnecessary layout of a pattern.

Don't fail to check up a layout when completed.

Don't make the mistake of subtracting the finish allowance from the diameter of a hole instead of from the radius.

PATTERN 12

LATHE LEG

Features presented:
A pattern layout
Pattern construction
Band-sawing
Application of a templet
Figure 116 is the drawing of a cast iron lathe leg.

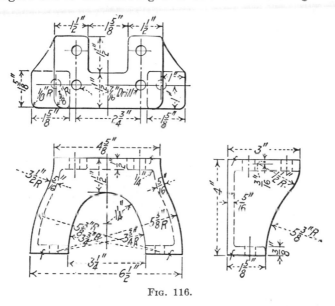

FIG. 116.

The leg casting is made up of a web, a flange, two ribs and two bolt lugs, as shown by the layout of the pattern in Fig. 115. Teh making of the pattern affords a good lesson in the use of the band-saw, for with the exception of rounding the corners,

111

the shaping of the pattern is practically completed upon this machine.

Stock required: $\frac{3}{4} \times 3 \quad \times 5\frac{1}{2}$ inches Flange
$1 \quad \times 3 \quad \times 9$ inches Ribs
$\frac{1}{2} \times 4\frac{1}{2} \times 7\frac{1}{2}$ inches Web
$\frac{5}{8} \times 1\frac{3}{4} \times 7$ inches Bolt Lugs

ORDER OF OPERATIONS

Dress no material to a width or length dimension.

1. Transfer from the *layout* Fig. 115 to flange stock the proportions of the rabbets, then dress the rabbets *C* to shape.

2. Draft the *inside* surface of the flange, then glue the stock for the ribs and the flange together. If the joint surfaces are pressed together and rubbed, the material need not be clamped together while the glue is drying.

3. Plane the edge of the material which is to receive the *web*, square to the face of the flange. The outlines of the ribs and the rabbets *D, are to be laid out upon the opposite edge of the material.*

4. Scribe the center line about the flange and gage a line indicating the amount of finish allowed upon the surface of the flange as at *A*, Fig. 115. The *position of the ribs* is fixed by the location of the center of radii *B* upon the extension of the gage line beyond the limit of the material as shown.

5. Saw the inside shape of the ribs to their outline. Draft is provided by *tilting* the saw table. Dress out the fillets *E*. Remove the saw marks from the inside surface of the ribs with coarse sandpaper.

6. Saw out the rabbets *D*. Figure 117 shows the pattern at the completion of this work.

7. Plane the web material to required *thickness and glue to the ribs and the flange.* The stock size of the web material will make projections of the web beyond the limits of the glued up work.

8. Get out the lug material *F in one piece* and fit it into place as shown by the broken lines in Fig. 117. The lugs are then shaped by the same *sawing operation* that reduces the pattern to form.

9. Dress the projecting edges of the web flush with the face of the flange and lug material.

10. Saw the outside shape of the ribs. Figure 118 shows how the work will appear when the outside of the ribs has been

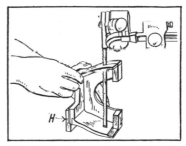

FIG. 117.—The pattern in course of construction.

FIG. 118.—Work ready for the final sawing operation.

sawed to shape. It also shows the layout upon the various surfaces of the pattern completed and ready to be sawed.

As the face of the ribs is curved, the profile of the ribs cannot be laid out directly upon this surface, but it is easily transferred to it from a paper templet. Cut the paper to the length of the surface *G*, then lay out the side view of the pattern upon it. The difference between the height of the pattern and the length of the templet is added to the 5⅜-inch radius. This will make an approximation close enough for this outline.

FIG. 119.—Sawing the pattern to its side view shape.

11. Order of sawing operations: Saw the elliptical opening in the *web*. Saw the rectangular opening in the *flange*. Saw

8

the work to its *side view*. This operation requires that the work be supported by a piece attached to the face of the flange as shown at *H*, Fig. 119.

Caution.—*Never attempt to saw to shape* an overhanging portion of a piece of work that is not supported in *direct line with the blade of the saw*. The failure to strictly adhere to this practice may result in *serious injury*.

12. Round the corners of the pattern and reinforce the joints with brads.

QUESTIONS

1. What is understood by counter-sawing?

2. For what purpose is the spoke-shave used?

3. What is understood by the term lateral surface?

4. What machine may be used to remove the surplus waste material from the cavity of semicircular core-boxes?

5. What tools may be used to dress to shape the surface of semicircular core-boxes?

6. On what principle is the core-box plane constructed?

7. For what purposes is the rabbet-plane used?

8. How does the bit of a rabbet-plane differ from the bit of a jack-plane?

9. How is the size of a rabbet-plane specified?

10. Why may the accuracy of the surface of a semicircular core-cavity be tested with a square?

11. What is understood by the layout of a pattern?

12. Why is a layout of some patterns necessary?

13. Why is a layout necessary for the lathe leg pattern?

14. What are the principle features presented by the lathe leg pattern?

15. What should be avoided in whetting the blade of a spoke-shave.

PATTERN 13

BELL-CRANK

Features presented:
The end-lap
Application of templet
Sandpapering
Supplementary patterns
Figure 120 is the drawing of a cast steel bell-crank.

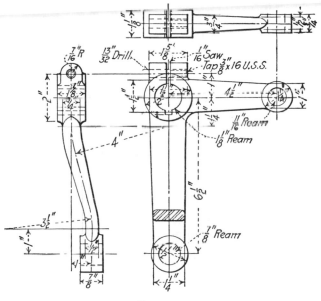

Fig. 120.

The material is joined together as shown in Fig. 121. This method of joining is known as the *end-lap*. The end-lap is made on a saw-bench. The two arms of the pattern lie in

115

the direction of the grain of wood, and therefore have the advantage of its *maximum strength.*

Make a layout of the pattern as shown in Fig. 122. The layout needed is to aid in determining the dimensions of

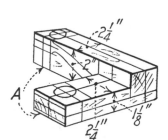

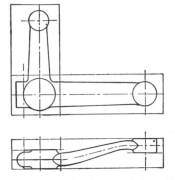

Fig. 121.—Method of gluing up the material for the bell-crank pattern.

Fig. 122.—The layout of the bell-crank pattern.

the required material and in the proportioning of the lap-joint.

Stock required: $2\frac{1}{8} \times 2\frac{3}{8} \times 9\frac{1}{4}$ inches
$1\frac{1}{4} \times 2\frac{3}{8} \times 6\frac{3}{4}$ inches

ORDER OF OPERATIONS

1. Plane the two pieces of material to the width and thickness shown in Fig. 121, then make the joint.

2. Glue parts together. The thickness given is a required pattern dimension, therefore the joint should be *tested before gluing,* in order to see that the surfaces *A* of the pieces lie in one plane.

3. Square up the outer edges of the pieces, and lay out the work from these surfaces.

4. Figure 123 shows the work at the completion of operation 4.

The material has been reduced as at *B* to the thickness of the bosses. The centers of the bosses have been located, and their circumferences scribed, as shown.

5. Upon the inside edge *C* of the material, lay out the thickness of the arms. The thickness of the offset arm may be traced from a paper or wood templet, or laid out directly upon the material.

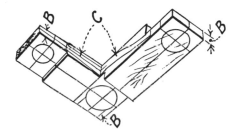

Fig. 123.—The thickness of the arms laid out and ready to be sawed.

6. Saw the work to this outline.

7. Figure 124 shows the work at the completion of operation 7.

The material has been sawed and dressed to the thickness of the arms, and the shape of the arms laid out.

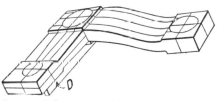

Fig. 124.—The layout of the arms and bosses completed and the work ready to be sawed to this outline.

8. Saw the work to this outline. Attach a piece as at *D*, to support the work while performing this operation.

9. Dress the bosses to shape, and round the edge of the arms as shown by the *cross-section* of one of the arms. Use the *spoke-shave* for this work. Figure 125 illustrates how a strip of sandpaper is used in finishing the rounded edge of the arms.

A cross-section or a sectional surface is a view of a casting
which is represented as cut through in some definite plane, the
cut face being presented to the eye.

FIG. 125.—Sandpapering the rounded edges of the bell-crank pattern.

Supplementary Pattern.—Frequently a note on the drawing
will specify that the opposite or *left-hand* pattern to that
shown by the drawing is wanted. If the *left-hand* pattern
of the bell-crank is to be made, the short arm should extend
to the left instead of to the right, as shown.

> Study the possibilities of the power-driven
> tools and save time and energy.

PATTERN 14

TOOL-REST SLIDE

Features presented:
  Giving greater strength to a pattern by the arrangement of the core-print
  Arranging a core-print so as to simplify the construction of the core-box
  Proportioning a core-print so as to balance a core
Figure 126 is the drawing of a cast iron tool-rest slide.

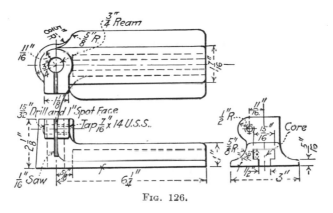

Fig. 126.

The casting is made up of a flanged body, a conical shaped boss and a clamping-lug. Extending through the body of the casting to within $\frac{5}{8}$ inch of the center of the boss, is a cored tee-head bolt slot.

The shape of the casting affords only one practical way in which to mold the pattern, and that is to part it *longitudinally, as shown in* Fig 127.

119

An end view layout of the pattern is shown in Fig. 128. The layout required is to make possible an illustration of the *proper proportions* of the core-print. The body of the pattern is made up of four pieces of material and the *cross-section* of

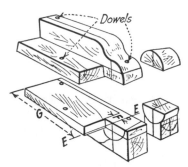

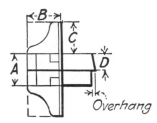

FIG. 127.—The drag and cope part of the pattern at different stages of completion.

FIG. 128.—The layout of the end view of the pattern.

these pieces is obtained from the layout. The layout is used for direct reference in proportioning the core-box.

Note how the *thickness* of the core-print is made to the width dimension, *A*, of the tee-head bolt slot. Making the core-print to this dimension has three advantages. First, it gives *added strength* to the pattern. Second, the core is made of *uniform thickness*, and will lay flat upon the core-plate when drying. Third, this arrangement of the core-print *simplifies* the construction of the core-box.

When a core lying horizontally in a mold receives its entire support from along one side, as in this case, the core-print portion is to *outweigh, or overbalance* that portion of the core which is surrounded by the molten metal. As the tee-head bolt-slot core extends into the mold $\frac{7}{8}$ inch, the print is to extend $1\frac{1}{8}$ *inch* from the face of the pattern.

Stock required: $\frac{5}{8} \times 2\frac{1}{2} \times 15$ inches $\bigg\}$ Body of pattern
$1\frac{1}{8} \times 1\frac{1}{4} \times 15$ inches $\bigg\}$
$1\frac{1}{4} \times 1\frac{1}{2} \times 4\frac{1}{4}$ inches Boss

ORDER OF OPERATIONS

1. Dress the material for the body of the pattern to the required dimensions *B, C* and *D*, Fig. 128 then glue the pieces together, as shown in Fig. 129.

2. Separate the material at the middle of its length. Set the dowel-pins at about the locations shown, Fig. 127.

3. Scribe center line *E* and lay off the dimension *F*, which is the distance from the center line of the boss to the end of the core-print.

4. Dress this end of the core-print to shape. (*Refer to the information on overhang given the cope half of core-prints, page 94.*)

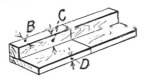

Fig. 129.—The glued up stock for the body of the pattern.

Fig. 130.—The boss and its attached clamping-lug partially shaped and ready to be secured to the body of the pattern.

5. Lay out the shape of the boss end of the pattern. Figure 127, shows the drag part of the pattern laid out.

6. Dress the work to dimension *G*.

7. Saw the boss end of the pattern to shape. *Do not dress to the exact outline.* The cope half of the pattern, shows the work at this stage of completion.

8. Lay out and dress to shape the projecting portion of the boss as shown in Fig. 130. The two halves of this part of the boss is shown in Fig. 127 opposite the surfaces to which they are to be attached.

9. Attach the parts and dress this end of the pattern to shape.

10. Dress the body of the pattern to the required cross-section.

CORE-BOX FOR THE TOOL-REST SLIDE PATTERN

Features presented:
Core-box construction

Stock required: 1 × 2½ × 13 inches   Frame
                 ⅞ × 4½ × 10 inches   Bottom board
                 ⅝ × ⅞ × 8 inches   Strip *B*
                 ⅜ × ⅝ × 6 inches   Strip *A*

Figure 131 illustrates the core which forms the tee-head slot in the tool-rest slide casting and the frame in which the core is shaped.

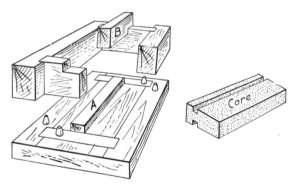

Fig. 131.—The core and core-box used in connection with the pattern for the tool-rest slide.

To better show the arrangement of the box, a section of one end, one side and a part of strip *B* has been cut away. The frame is shown above the bottom-board to which it is attached with dowels.

The depressions in the core are formed by the strips *A* and *B*. Strip *A* is attached to the bottom-board. Strip *B* is a rectangular loose strip. It is located and held in place by a notch cut in the end pieces of the frame. To give stiffness to strip *B*, it is proportioned so as to project about ½ inch above the frame as shown.

The relative position of the frame of the core-box to the bottom-board is to be indicated, by the *outline* of the inside of the frame, being traced upon the *surface of the board.*

The location of strip *B* upon the frame is to be indicated with a *tally-mark,* a tally-mark is easily made by duplicating a number as 1-1—2-2 or 3-3, etc.

All parts and pieces of the core-box is to *stamped or marked* with the number of the pattern.

When making the core, strip *B* is held in position while the box is rammed up. The strip is then removed, and this face of the core laid upon the core plate. The bottom-board is then lifted off and the frame removed.

For construction of frame, *refer to instruction given with the core-frame for Pattern 9, page 97.*

PATTERN 15

STEADY-REST

Features presented:
  Simplifying the parting of a mold by the use of a core
  Registering a core
  The compass-saw
  Strengthening a fragile section of a pattern
Figure 132 is the drawing of a cast iron steady-rest.

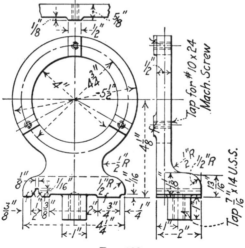

Fɪɢ. 132.

The casting is made up of a web, a flange, a boss and three pads.

Dry sand cores are used not only to produce holes, cavities and the interior shape of castings, but are very frequently employed to form a *plane or straight parting of a mold.*

124

This feature is presented by the pattern for the steady-rest. Notice how a 1-inch diameter *boss* extends out from the depressed surface of the face of the flange, then imagine how the parting of the mold would have to be formed if the face of the pattern were made like that of the casting.

This objectionable parting is eliminated if a core-print is used, as shown in Fig. 133 and the face of the flange formed by *a dry sand core.* To assure a *correct setting* of the core in the mold, the print is made to extend as at *A*, about ¼ inch beyond the flange as shown.

To *avoid placing* the core in the mold in any other position than that intended, one corner of the print at *B is chamfered*

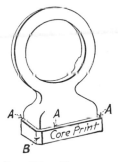 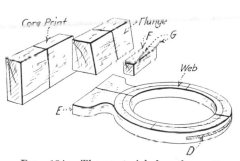

FIG. 133.—The pattern for the steady-rest.

FIG. 134.—The material for the pattern partially shaped and ready to be attached together.

as shown, and the corresponding corner of the core *C*, Fig. 137, shaped similarly. This is called *marking a core.* The raised surface *H* of the core does not extend the full width of the core. By making the raised surface the width of the flange, no core-print projection of this shape beyond the flang is necessary.

No attention is given the *V-shaped* slot in the face of the flange; forming it requires a machine-shop operation. If the common allowance for machine-finish is made upon the surface of a groove, and this allowance leaves a very small groove to be made in the pattern, *no consideration is given the groove.*

Figure 134 illustrates the separated parts of the pattern. The flange and the core-print are shown opposite the surface of the web to which they are later attached.

The 4-inch hole through the web may be formed by one of three methods: sawing it out with a compass-saw, as

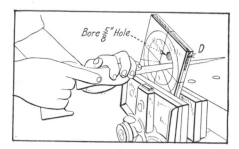

Fɪɢ. 135.—Sawing out the hole in the web with a compass-saw.

shown in Fig. 135, then dressing it to shape, or securing the web material to a face plate as shown in Fig. 136, and turning out the hole, or by making a joint in the material along

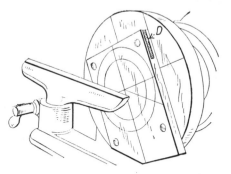

Fɪɢ. 136.—The web material mounted upon a face plate for the turning out of the hole.

the middle of its width and sawing out the hole, then, gluing it together.

Note: If a *tongue* is inserted in the web material, as at *D*, Fig. 136, it will *greatly strengthen* the short grain wood which occurs at this point in the web. It consists of a saw cut into which a strip is inserted and glued.

Stock required:

$\frac{5}{8}$ × 6	× $7\frac{1}{2}$ inches	Web
$1\frac{3}{8}$ × $1\frac{3}{4}$	× $4\frac{3}{4}$ inches	Flange
1 × $2\frac{1}{2}$	× $5\frac{1}{4}$ inches	Core-print
$\frac{5}{8}$ × $\frac{5}{8}$	× $3\frac{1}{2}$ inches	Fillet stock
$\frac{3}{8}$ × $\frac{3}{4}$	× 4 inches	Pads
$\frac{1}{4}$ × $1\frac{1}{2}$	× $6\frac{1}{2}$ inches	Tongue

ORDER OF OPERATIONS

1. Make the groove in the web material upon the circular-saw-bench, then get out the strip or tongue *D* and glue and clamp it in place. When the glue has dried, dress the web material to the required thickness and scribe the center lines.

If the enclosed waste material is to be turned out, mount the material upon a face plate as shown in Fig. 136. *Locate the center of rotation*, then scribe the center lines through this point.

2. Lay out the shape of the web and dress or turn the circular opening.

3. Saw and dress the outer edge of the web to shape. When the surfaces of two members of a pattern are to coincide, as the ends of the flange and edge of web, as at *E*, it is a good practice to make the length of the flange at this point a trifle full. This permits the ends of the flange to be dressed off to conform to the shape of the web after the parts are attached.

4. Dress the flange material to length and cross-section and attach it to the web. Fit and glue into the corner formed by the flange and the web, the piece of stock *F*; it is to form the $\frac{1}{2}$-inch fillet. Brads are driven in as at *G*, holding the piece in place while the glue is setting. The application of the wood fillet is made to this pattern in order that this *construction* may be applied if desired. Ordinarily, a leather fillet would be used.

5. Dress the ends of the flange material to conform to the shape of the web.

6. Dress the core-print to shape and attach. The *thickness* of the core-print is equal to the distance the boss extends out beyond the finished face of the flange.

7. Attach the three pads. The *end surfaces* of the pads are to leave their impression in the *drag*. (*Draft accordingly.*)

When the thickness of a core represents the length of a projection on a casting, as in the case of the boss, the shape of the projection should be so indicated on the face of the core-print by shellacking it the *color which denotes metal*.

CORE-BOX FOR THE STEADY-REST PATTERN

Features presented:

Core-box construction

Stock required: $1 \times 2\frac{1}{2} \times 12$ inches   Frame

$\frac{7}{8} \times 4\frac{1}{2} \times$ 9 inches   Bottom-board

$1\frac{1}{4} \times 1\frac{1}{4} \times 2\frac{1}{2}$ inches   Boss

Figure 137 illustrates the core for the steady-rest and the box in which the core is shaped. To better show the arrange-

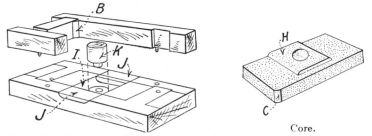

Core.

FIG. 137.—Core-box and core used in connection with the pattern for the steady-rest.

ment of the box and the bottom-board, one end of the frame and a section of one side has been cut away. The raised surface of the core *H* is formed by the depression *I* in the bottom-board.

If the drawing of the steady-rest has been carefully studied, it will have been observed that this depression does not occur at the *middle* of the length of the core. The hole through the core is formed by the boss *K*. The boss is attached to the bottom-board by a dowel ½ inch in diameter.

To check or verify by *observation* the arrangement of a core-box with the pattern, hold the box in its relative position to the pattern, then compare its outlines and the arrangement of the parts.

Cut out depression *I* the full width of the bottom-board; sandpaper it, then glue in the filling pieces *J*. In attaching the boss to the bottom-board, keep in mind *that its center* does not locate at the middle of the width of the core. The triangular block *B* chamfers the corner of the core at *C* and *marks the core for its correct setting in the mold.*

PATTERN 16

SHACKLE

Features presented.
Construction

Figure 138 is the drawing of a cast steel shackle. The casting is composed of a double and a single boss united by two ribs; the ribs are connected by a web.

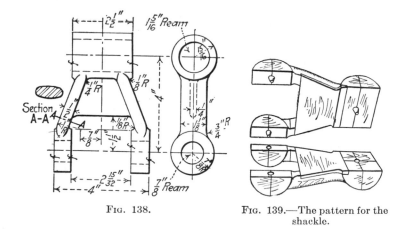

FIG. 138.   FIG. 139.—The pattern for the
                                      shackle.

Unless otherwise instructed, *finished holes* in steel castings of 1½-*inch* diameter or less, will *be drilled.*

Figure 139 illustrates the pattern. Note how the grain of wood of the web is laid in a *transverse direction* to that of the ribs. This construction gives greater strength to the pattern.

Stock required: 1⅛ × 4½ × 13 inches   Body
           3/16 × 2⅛ × 9 inches   Web

ORDER OF OPERATIONS

1. Arrange the parting and set the dowels.

2. Dress the material to the greatest width of the pattern, then scribe the longitudinal and transverse center lines.

3. Upon each edge lay out the side view of the pattern, then dress the material tangent to the circumference of the bosses as shown, Fig. 140.

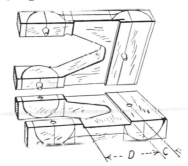

Fig. 140.—The pattern in process of making.

4. Upon each face of the material lay out the top view of the pattern.

5. Upon each edge lay out the depression which is to receive the web. Make distance C, about ¾ inch, and distance D about 2 inches.

6. Dress out the depression for the web.

7. Saw and dress to shape the inside surfaces of the ribs and double boss. Figure 140 illustrates the work at this stage of completion.

8. Attach the web.

9. Saw and dress the work to the outline of the bosses and ribs.

10. *Rescribe* those lines on the face of the material which were destroyed by the previous operation, then saw and dress the work to this shape of the pattern.

11. Dress to shape the lateral surface of the boss which lies between the ribs.

PATTERN 17

BRACKET

Features presented:

Construction

Using a core-print to protect a pattern from being distorted by the ramming of the sand

Figure 141 is the drawing of a cast iron bracket.

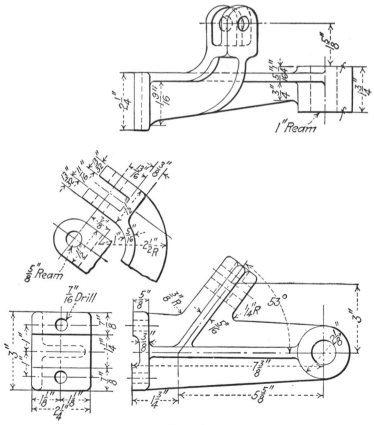

Fig. 141.

132

The pattern for the bracket is illustrated in Fig. 142 and the separated parts in Fig. 143. The ears *C* will be molded in the cope; this arrangement necessitates that a parting in the pattern be made at *D*.

What often appears as a difficult pattern to make will, after a little effort on the part of the imagination, resolve

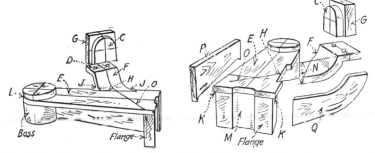

FIG. 142.—The pattern for the bracket.

FIG. 143.—The pattern in process of construction.

itself into a number of *simply shaped parts*. This is true of the bracket casting, for if each member is considered separately as it is shown, the construction of the pattern becomes a simple problem.

The web is made up of two pieces of material; the main portion of the web *E* supports the boss and the flange; the curved portion of the web *F* supports the ears *C*. The ears *C* have a small bearing surface upon the web, and the ramming of the mold will likely *distort them*. To prevent this distortion, a *core-print G secures the ears together and keeps them in place.*

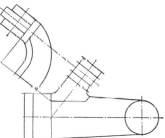

FIG. 144.—The layout of the pattern for the bracket.

A partial layout of the pattern, as shown in Fig. 144, is required. From it is obtained the dimensions of the material for web *F*. Attention is called to the fact that the web *F*, which supports the cars, is set about $\frac{1}{4}$ inch into the web E, at H. This is done to strengthen the joint and to allow stock for the fillets J.

Stock required:

$\frac{7}{16} \times 3\frac{1}{2} \times 9$ inches	Web E
$1\frac{1}{2} \times 2\frac{3}{8} \times 4$ inches	Web F
$\frac{3}{4} \times 2\frac{1}{4} \times 3\frac{1}{2}$ inches	Flange
$1\frac{1}{2} \times 2\frac{1}{2} \times 2\frac{1}{2}$ inches	Boss
$\frac{1}{2} \times 2\frac{1}{2} \times 2\frac{1}{2}$ inches	Boss
$\frac{1}{2} \times 1\frac{3}{4} \times 3\frac{3}{4}$ inches	Ears
$1\frac{3}{16} \times 2\frac{1}{4} \times 2\frac{1}{4}$ inches	Core-print
$\frac{7}{16} \times 1\frac{3}{4} \times 6\frac{1}{2}$ inches	Rib P
$\frac{7}{16} \times 2\frac{1}{2} \times 5\frac{1}{2}$ inches	Rib Q

ORDER OF OPERATIONS

1. Prepare the material for the web E, then lay out the shape of this member. *Do not dress to shape.*

When the surfaces of two members of a pattern are to coincide, as the ends of the flange and the edges of the web, as at K, or the end of the web with the cylindrical surface of the boss as at L, the outline of the *edge* of the web should be made a *trifle full;* the web is then dressed off after the parts have been attached. Likewise, when a depression occurs in the surface of two members, as at M, the depression should be dressed out after the parts have been put together.

2. Dress to shape the opening H, which is to receive web F, then saw the web E to shape.

3. Web F is made by dressing a block to the required width and to the thickness N. Fit the block into the opening H, then scribe the center line O, and locate the position of the core-print. Lay out the outline of web F upon the edge surface of the material. *Do not dress web to shape.*

4. Dress the core-print G to shape and dowel it in place.

5. Dress the ears C to shape and attach to the core-print.

6. Saw and dress the web F to the shape laid out upon the edge surfaces of the material. Lay out the outline of web F upon the parting surface and saw and dress to this shape.

7. Glue webs E and F together, then dress out the fillets J.

8. Shape the two parts of the boss and the flange and attach parts to web E.

9. Fit the material for rib P into place, then dress to shape and attach. Fit the material for rib Q into place, then dress to shape and attach.

CORE-FRAME FOR THE BRACKET PATTERN

Features presented:

Band-sawing a core-frame to shape

Figure 145 shows the core-frame in course of making. The material should be about 2 inches greater in width and $3\frac{1}{2}$

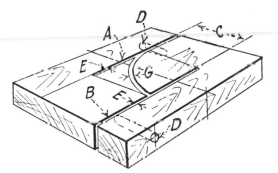

FIG. 145.—Core-frame used in connection with the pattern for the bracket.

inches greater in length, than the width and length dimensions of the core. The material is planed to the required *thickness* of the core, then the shape of the core laid out upon one face.

The lines A and B which represent the width of the core cavity C are gaged throughout the length of the material as shown. Dowel-pin holes are bored as at D.

Make saw cuts as represented by E along the *inside* of the line A and along the *outside* of the line B. The frame is separated by making a saw cut as indicated by G. Saw the core cavity to length dimension, sandpaper and insert the dowel-pins.

When cores are of approximately the dimensions required by this job, this type of core-frame may be used.

QUESTIONS

1. When is the end lap used?

2. What is the object in securing together with the lap-joint the material for the bell-crank pattern?

3. What is understood by the term cross-section of a casting?

4. For what purposes is the compass-saw used?

5. What is marking a core understood to mean?

6. Describe the operation of inserting the tongue in the web material of the steady-rest pattern.

7. What is the object in forming the face of the flange of the steady-rest casting with a dry sand core?

8. Describe two methods of forming the hole in the web material of the steady-rest pattern.

9. What features may be applied to prevent small loose parts or projections on a pattern being distorted by the ramming of the sand?

10. Describe a method of laying out and sawing to shape small rectangular core-frames.

> Looking and seeing are both distinct and different. You *"look"* with the eye, but *"see"* with the brain; make sure you *see* through the drawing before starting work upon the pattern.

PATTERN 18

TAIL STOCK

Features presented:
Construction
Loose piece feature
Scribing lines upon irregular surfaces
Application of templets
Application of counter sawing
Indicating the location of loose parts of patterns
Indicating where fillets are required in the casting
Figure 146 is the drawing of a cast iron tail stock.

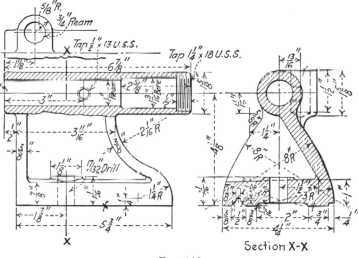

FIG. 146.

A longitudinal section of the barrel is given to more clearly show the interior of this member. The other view of the casting is that of a cross section along the line XX.

137

The pattern is molded upon its side. The clamping-lugs, parted from the barrel, so that it may lift off with the cope.

If a slight clearance depression of $\frac{1}{16}$ inch or less is required throughout the length of a finished surface, as in the *face of the flange*, and it would require the use of a dry sand core or a part of the pattern to be made loose in order to mold the pattern, the surface of the casting is made plane; and *the depression machined out*.

The layout of the pattern required is shown by Fig. 147. It gives the names of the various members of the casting.

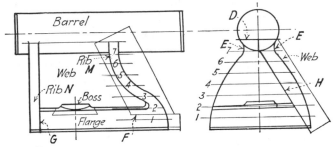

Fig. 147.—The layout of the pattern for the tail-stock.

When a projection occurs (*as the boss*) on a casting at a point beyond the limit of the parting of the mold, *the loose piece feature* in pattern construction is applied.

To permit the *boss* upon the top surface of the flange to *remain in the sand until the withdrawal* of the body of the pattern, it is made a loose piece. It is located and held in place by the *tongue, B*, Fig. 148. The tongue is held in place by its beveled edges engaging a corresponding bevel upon the sides of slot as at *C*. This is commonly called a *dovetail tongue*. By giving a slant of about $\frac{3}{4}$ inch to 12 inches to each edge of the tongue, it will instantly release itself from the body of the pattern. The tongue affords the means whereby the *loose piece may be drawn and lifted out of the mold*.

Whenever a loose piece is to be drawn and taken out through a narrow cavity of a mold, as in the present case, the dovetail feature should be applied. When considering the loose piece feature, be sure that the *space* into which the loose piece is to be drawn will easily *permit of this operation.*

Carefully study, in conjunction with the layout, the construction of the pattern as illustrated by Fig. 148. *Note* the arrangement of the joints between the adjacent pieces of material. Note how the joint between the barrel and the body

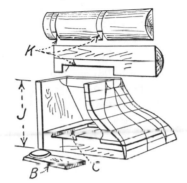

Fig. 148.—The pattern in process of construction.

of the pattern is made along the line D, Fig. 147. Line D is located by the point of *tangency* between the radii of the fillets E and the circumference of the barrel.

In getting out the material, keep in mind that the pattern is sawed to the shape of the end view, and that ample waste ($\frac{1}{2}$ inch) is to be allowed for this operation.

Stock required:
$1\frac{1}{4} \times 4\frac{3}{4} \times 6$ inches Flange
$\frac{7}{8} \times 5 \times 6\frac{1}{4}$ inches Web
$1\frac{3}{8} \times 4\frac{3}{4} \times 4\frac{3}{4}$ inches Rib M
$\frac{1}{2} \times 4\frac{3}{4} \times 4\frac{3}{4}$ inches Rib N
$1 \times 2 \times 17\frac{1}{2}$ inches Barrel
$\frac{5}{16} \times 1\frac{3}{4} \times 6$ inches Tongue and boss
$1\frac{3}{4} \times 2\frac{1}{4} \times 2\frac{1}{2}$ inches Clamping-lug
$\frac{3}{8} \times 2\frac{1}{4} \times 2\frac{1}{2}$ inches Clamping-lug

ORDER OF OPERATIONS

1. Make the rabbet F, Fig. 147, in flange material which is to receive the stock for the rib M, then plane flange to its diminishing thickness.

2. Dress out the slot C in flange ($\frac{3}{16}$ *inch deep*), which is to receive the tongue B. Fit the tongue snugly into the slot. Dress the end of the flange at G, to which is to be attached the stock for the rib N.

3. Glue parts together. Use brads to temporarily hold the parts together while the glue is setting. Place a protecting strip of about $\frac{1}{2}$ inch thickness between the brad heads and the work. The strip will permit the *withdrawal* of the brads.

4. Dress the edge surfaces of the work square to the face of the flange and to its greatest parallel width (*about* $4\frac{5}{8}$ *inches*). Upon the edge of the work which is to be the drag side of the pattern, lay out the shape of the rib M, then saw the rib to the required thickness.

5. Sandpaper the inside surfaces of the rib M; this operation is more easily accomplished at this time than if done after the web material is attached.

6. On the waste material cut from the outside of the rib M, locate and scribe a line which will correspond in location to line H, of the layout. Dress the material to this line, then replace the material upon the rib and transfer line H to the rib. Line H may also be scribed between the given points by the method illustrated with Pattern 29, page 204, or by an angle plate as illustrated in Fig. 235, page 205.

7. Separate the work along the line H, then attach the web material. Use brads as previously explained, to hold parts together while the glue is setting.

8. Guiding the saw by the curved surface of the rib M, saw off the protruding end of the web material. Dress and sandpaper this surface, then saw the body of the pattern to its required height J, Fig. 148.

9. The curved surface of the rib M will not easily permit the end view shape of the pattern to be made directly upon it; therefore, a paper templet, as shown in Fig. 149, of the end view shape is made and the outline of the pattern traced from it. The shape of the end view of the pattern being the same each side of the center line, a templet of one half the end view is sufficient.

The shape of the templet is developed by dividing the height of the body of the pattern, as shown by the layout into a number of equal parts, as 1-2-3, etc., then squaring these lines across the surface of the rib M. The spacings of these lines are transferred to a piece of heavy paper while it is held, and caused to conform to the curved surface of the rib.

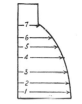

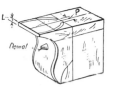

FIG. 149.—Paper templet.　　　FIG. 150.—The clamping-lug in course of shaping.

The edge of paper which represents the center line of the templet must coincide with the center line of the pattern. Transfer to the paper, from the corresponding lines of the layout, the half width of the pattern at these stations 1-2-3, etc., and connect the points obtained by a line drawn free hand or with the aid of a French curve. Cut the paper to this outline, then trace its shape upon the curved surface of the rib, as shown in Fig. 148.

10. Turn the barrel portion of the pattern. The barrel is shown in Fig. 148 above the surface of the body to which it is later attached. To facilitate the laying out and sawing to shape of the joint K, the *barrel is made in halves*.

11. Saw the body of the pattern to its end view shape, attach the barrel, then dress out the fillets E.

The material from which the clamping-lug is sawed is shown in Fig. 150. It is fitted into place, doweled, then dressed to required height, as shown.

To avoid the thin short grain wood that would occur at L, if the lug were made from one piece of material, it is made up of two pieces, the grain of the pieces lying in a transverse direction. The piece which forms the thin edge is about ⅜ inch thick.

Ample stock (*about* 1½ *inches*) is allowed beyond the limit of the lug, that the work may be *firmly held* while the lug is being sawed to shape.

Lay out the top and side views of the lug upon the material, then saw to the top view of the lug.   In performing this operation, *do not complete the entire outline of the lug*, but allow ¼ inch of stock to remain, as at *P*, to hold the material together. The sawing to shape of the side view separates the lug from the waste.

12. Saw the clamping-lug to its top view, then its side views.

The fillet connecting the lower part of the lug, with the surface of the web, is to be dressed to conform to the convexed surface of the lug.   The surface of the ribs *M* and *N* Figure 147 that is above the joint line *H* is to be coped; *it is to be drafted accordingly.*   Whenever a part of a pattern as in the case of the lug is made loose from the body, its position should be *plainly indicated.*   The general practice is to place the parts in position, then with a small marking brush *apply a line of shellac,* of a contrasting color, along the corner formed by the intersecting surfaces.   The marking not only calls attention to the fact that a part of the pattern is required at this location, but also, that the molder is to finish the mold in such a way as to form a *fillet in the corner of the casting.*

PATTERN 19

YOKE

Features presented:

Construction

Strengthening a yoke-shaped pattern with a tie-piece

Casting in a tie-piece to prevent the distortion of the casting

Stopping-off a part of a pattern which is not a part of the required casting

Figure 151 is the drawing of a cast iron yoke.

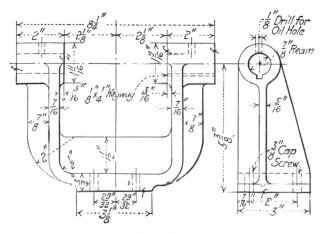

FIG. 151.

The pattern is parted along one face of the web. It is shown in course of construction in Fig. 152. The two bosses *A* are interconnected by a ¾-inch diameter tie-piece, *B*.

The tie-piece *B* is a pattern feature; no reference is made to it on the drawing. *A tie-piece* greatly adds to the strength

143

of a pattern of *this shape.* It is easily stopped off if it is not desired to have it function in the casting.

Stopping off is the term applied to the operation of *filling in with sand* a depression left by a pattern. When a tie-piece is not intended to be cast in, it is marked *"stop off."*

In the production of a yoke shaped casting, it is good practice to cast the tie-piece in, otherwise, *little or no contraction*

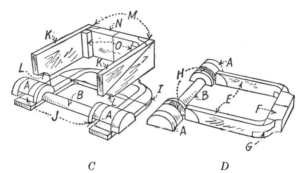

C   *D*

Fig. 152.—The drag and the cope part of the yoke pattern in process of construction.

will have taken place between the open ends. This would cause a *distorted casting.* The tie-piece is later removed from the casting.

The separated parts of the drag half of the pattern are illustrated at *C,* and the cope half of the pattern at *D,* Fig. 152. The bosses are cut out as at *H* to receive the ribs *E.* The bosses *A* of the drag part of the pattern are cut out as at *J,* to receive the web.

The ribs *K* of the drag are rigidly attached to the web. No advantage would be derived by letting the ribs into the bosses, therefore they are dressed to fit, as at *L,* the convex surface of the bosses. A butt-joint, as at *M,* is used to join the flange *N* and the ribs *K.* The fillet material at *O* is glued in place, then dressed to shape.

A partial layout of the pattern, as shown in Fig. 153, will aid in the work.

The information given with Pattern 15, page 127, regarding the use of fillets, advised the application of leather fillets unless the requirements of the pattern made the application of wood fillets desirable. This pattern illustrates one of the uses of a

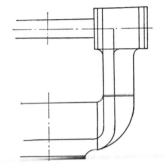

FIG. 153 — The layout of the pattern for the yoke.

wood fillet. In this case, the wood fillet *reinforces the pattern at this point.*

To assemble flange *N* and ribs *K*, attach the flange to the web, *temporarily, with brads.* Fit the ribs over the bosses, as at *L*, and glue the ribs to the flange. Glue in the blocks *O*. When the glue has set, the frame thus formed is removed, dressed to shape, and returned to its place and attached.

The Cornering Tool.—The cornering tool as illustrated in Fig. 154, is used for rounding the corners of patterns. It is a

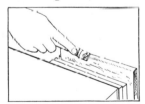

FIG. 154.—Rounding a corner with a cornering-tool.

flat steel bar formed and ground at each end to produce an elliptical cutting edge. The shape of the cutting edge permits a cut to be taken in either direction.

10

PATTERN 20

SEPARATOR

Features presented:
Locating a core above or below the parting of the mold
Tail or stop-off core-prints
Making tail core-prints
Core-box construction
Figure 155 is the drawing of a cast iron separator.

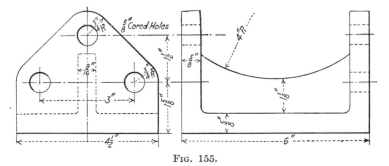

FIG. 155.

The casting is made up of a web, two flanges and a rib. The drawing *specifies that the holes in the flanges are to be cored.*

Figure 156 illustrates the pattern. Rabbet-joints secure the flanges to the web. The rib is fitted in between the two flanges. The core-prints, *tail-prints*, visible in the illustration are indicated by *A* and *B*. The *shape* of the core-prints does not convey any idea as to the shape of that portion of the cores which forms the *holes in the casting.* The cross section of the mold, Fig. 157 illustrates this feature.

The shape of the portion of the core which forms the hole through the flange is *below the parting* of the mold, at *C*; the core-print portion of the core is indicated by *D*. The core-

146

print not only forms a seat for the core, but it leaves an opening through which the core is *lowered to its proper location.* The shape of the tail, or portion *D* of the core, is made to correspond to this part of the core-print. It is the means

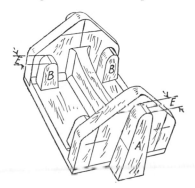

Fig. 156.—The pattern for the separator.

by which the core is *set and held in place* and the core-print depression *closed or stopped off.*

Make the dimensions *E*, Fig. 156, of the core-prints equal to the thickness of the flange. This proportion makes a good

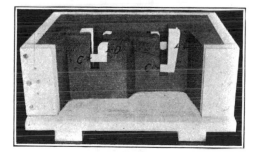

Fig. 157.—Sectional view of the drag part of the mold for the separator casting.

bearing for the core. Make the slant of the sides and the face of the core-prints *1 inch in 12 inches.*

Figure 158 illustrates a way whereby a number of tail core-prints is made from one piece of material. The width of the stock will depend upon the thickness of the core-prints and the number required. Allowance is also to be made for the saw cuts in the separation of the prints.

At each end of the material lay out upon each edge, the shape of the width dimension of the print. Dress material to

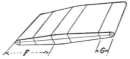

FIG. 158.—The core-prints in process of shaping.

this shape, then sandpaper. The prints are more easily sand-papered in one piece than when separated.

Saw and dress to the length dimension *F-G*. Separate the prints, then dress the face surface, giving it the required *slant*. The slant is given the face surface of the core-print to *facilitate the setting of the core.*

Fillet the corners of the pattern, then fit and attach the core-prints.

CORE-BOXES

Figure 159 illustrates the two core-boxes required. To facilitate the dressing to shape of the core cavity, the depth of the box is made up of two thicknesses of material.

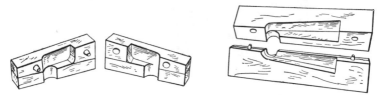

FIG. 159.—The core-boxes used in connection with the pattern for the separator.

The slant on the face of the box is dressed after the parts are assembled and the *halves doweled together.* Allow about 1½ inches of stock between the core cavity and the ends of the box, and about ¾ inch between the core cavity and the sides of the box.

PATTERN 21

BRACKET

Features presented:
  Attaching loose pieces
  Loose dowels
  Sectional layout of a core-box
  Shaping members which have a diminishing thickness
Figure 160 is the drawing of a cast iron bracket.

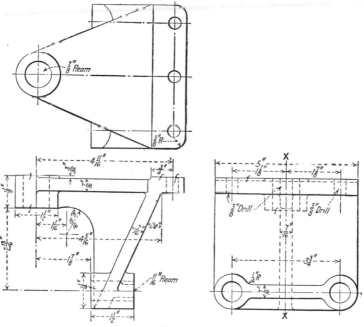

FIG. 160.

The shape of the casting suggests that the pattern be molded in the position in which it is shown, Fig. 161. The adjacent surfaces of the web are formed by a dry sand core; the rib-connected bosses A *are made a loose piece.*

The loose piece A is held in place during the early stage of the molding operation by the two protruding *loose dowels, B.* The *loose dowels* are made a *sliding fit* in the holes so that they may be *easily withdrawn.*

The pattern is molded in the usual way. When the ramming of the sand has reached the loose piece, the sand is firmly

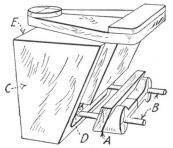

Fig. 161.—The pattern for the bracket casting.

tucked about this piece and the *dowel-pins drawn out* from the face of the core-print. The ramming of the mold is then carried to completion.

Fig. 162.—Sectional view of the drag part of the mold for the bracket casting.

The loose piece makes it possible to draw the body of the pattern from the sand.

Figure 162 illustrates a cross section of the bracket mold; the body of the pattern has been drawn. The loose piece, as shown at *A*, is now drawn back into the depression left vacant by the body, and taken out.

The portion of the web to which the rib-connected bosses are attached is made a part of the loose piece. The shoulder formed as at *D*, prevents the loose piece from being *dislodged after the dowels have been removed*.

The core-print is made to extend about ⅜ inch beyond the web. The face of the core-print is made in line with the center of the boss, *as at E*.

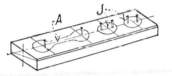

FIG. 163.—Method of arranging the material when shaping the bosses *A* and *J*.

One half of the boss impression as *at F*, Fig. 162, is delivered by the pattern. The other half of the boss impression is formed in the core.

An easy way to make the rib-connected bosses of the loose piece *A* of the pattern and the bosses *J* for the core-box,

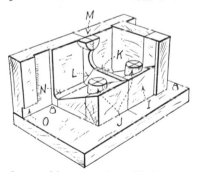

FIG. 164.—The core-box used in connection with the pattern for the bracket.

is shown in Fig. 163. Dress up a strip 14 inches long, whose angle of diminishing thickness is the same as the surface to which the bosses are to be attached. Saw the strip into two lengths, and place the lengths together as shown. This makes a piece of uniform thickness which facilitates the shaping of these members.

Figure 164 illustrates the core-box. One side and one end have been removed to better show the interior of the box. Make a cross sectional layout of the pattern along the line XX Fig. 160. The cross-section of the core-print portion of the pattern will be the cross-section of the interior of the core-box. *They must agree exactly.*

The core-box consists of a rectangular frame, a bottom-board, and a block I, to which is attached the bosses J. The rib K is separated along the line L. One portion of the rib is attached to the block. The other portion is made a part of the half boss, M, and is attached to the side of the box.

To provide stock from which to dress out the fillet, N, a rabbet is sawed in the side of the box, as at O, and the strip glued to block I. Block I is attached to the bottom-board. Strip N and block I can be made from the same piece of wood, but are more easily and quickly made as described.

Reminders

Don't forget that dowel-pins are to be set as far apart as the work will permit.

Don't set dowel pins in the drag part of a pattern.

Don't forget that loose dowel-pins are to be made a sliding fit.

Don't provide bottom-boards for core-frames unless necessary.

Don't forget to mark all loose pieces of a pattern with the pattern number.

Don't fail to indicate with a tally-mark the location of loose pieces.

PATTERN 22

HOPPER

Features presented:
 Laying out the joint surfaces of materials which meet
 at an angle and are inclined to the horizontal plane
 Stopping-off a core-print depression
 Supporting fragile patterns to prevent their distortion
 during the ramming of the mold

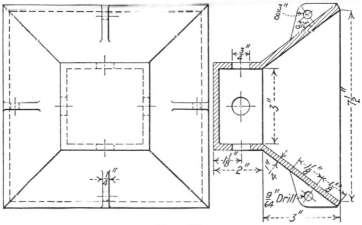

FIG. 165.

Figure 165 is the drawing of a cast iron hopper. The hopper
portion terminates in a square base or box section, which has
an opening in each side.

The pattern is to be molded with the base in the drag.
The interior of the hopper portion will be *coped out*. The
inside of the base will be formed by a *dry sand core*.

The inside of the casting might be formed in green sand
with the exception of the four openings through the walls

153

of the base. The pattern for this type of mold would be substantially as shown by the cross-section view of the casting. This would be a *fragile pattern*, and would be easily *broken or distorted* during the ramming up of the mold. To *avoid this objectionable feature*, it is assumed that the base portion of the pattern is to be a solid piece. This necessitates the coping out of the hopper portion.

FIG. 166.—Sectional view of the drag part of the mold for the hopper casting.

The four openings in the base afford the means of supporting the core. It is not always practical to form a core so that it will *stop off*, or fill the entire depression left by the core-print. This feature is illustrated by a cross-section of a mold, Fig. 166. The core is shown in place. The upper parts of the core-print depressions *A* are not occupied by the core, but through them the core is lowered into place. This space is then *stopped off by filling it with sand as at B*. Core-print depressions in the cope part of a mold may be stopped off in a like manner.

The pattern is shown in Fig. 167. For the guidance of the molder, the general practice is to apply the *core-print* color only to that surface of the *core-print* at *C*, which represents the part of its depression *to be occupied by the core*.

The sides of hopper patterns of this character may be either joined by a *miter or a butt-joint*. The miter-joint is used in the pattern described.

The angle and inclination of the joint surfaces occurring at the corners of the hopper between the sides pieces may be found as follows. Make a cross section layout of one of the flaring sides as shown in Fig. 168.

The width of the material used is represented by D. The flare of the sides is represented by E. The lesser length of the inside surface of the sides is represented by G.

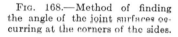

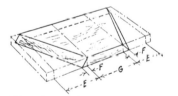

Fig. 167.—The pattern for the hopper.

Fig. 168.—Method of finding the angle of the joint surfaces occurring at the corners of the sides.

The distance F is used to find the inclination of the joint surface to the face of the material.

Figure 169 illustrates one of the side pieces dressed to shape. The outline of the waste removed in performing this operation is shown in broken lines.

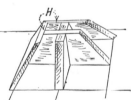

Fig. 169.—One of the sides as it is laid out upon and cut from the material.

Fig. 170.—Method of attaching the sides together.

Dress the material to the required thickness and width and at the center of its length lay off the distance G.

With the distance E find the angle of the joint across the inside face of the material. With the distance F, find the inclination of the joint surface as it is laid out upon the two edge surfaces of the material. *The shaping of the joint surfaces is a good job for the universal saw bench.*

The side pieces as indicated by *H*, Fig. 170, are more easily glued and nailed together if a support is made and used as illustrated. The support is made to correspond to the *height* and to the *angle* of the inside of the hopper. This support may be used to prevent possible distortion of the hopper portion of the pattern during the ramming of the mold. Distortion may occur when patterns are made rather fragile, through the use of thin material.

CORE-BOX FOR THE HOPPER

The core-box for the hopper as illustrated in Fig. 171, consists of a frame of the usual construction.

About the inside of the frame, blocks are arranged as shown,

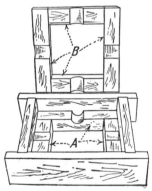

in which are dressed the cavities that form the cylindrical projections on the sides of the core.

To permit the removal of the box from the core, a parting in the blocks is made through the axes of the cavities. Blocks *A* are attached in place. Blocks *B* are attached together in the form of a frame. Attaching blocks *B* together gives a smaller number of parts to be taken care of.

FIG. 171.—The core-box used in connection with the hopper pattern.

The Core.—To make the core, blocks *B* are set in the frame and firmly held in place while the core is rammed up. The blocks are then removed and the space left vacant filled up with *green sand*, which is struck off level with the top of the box. A core-plate is then placed upon this surface and the box rolled over and removed from the core. *The green sand supports the cylindrical projections of the core during the drying process.*

PATTERN 23

BRACKET

Features presented:
  Laminated construction
  The cake or cover core
  Bedding in a pattern
  Core-box construction
Figure 172 is the drawing of a cast iron bracket.
Figure 173 illustrates the pattern.

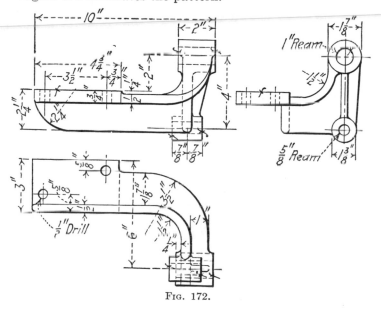

FIG. 172.

The casting is made up of a flange A; rib. B; bosses, C and D; the bosses are connected by the rib E.

The pattern will be molded with the boss D in the drag. This position of molding presents what is commonly called the *cake or cover core method.*

157

The cover core.   The cover core feature, as applied to this pattern, makes it possible to secure the boss D to the core-print F. The core-print is attached to the rib B of the pattern.

During the operation of ramming up the drag, the core-print with the attached boss is drawn out. The depression left vacant by the core-print is then closed with a dry sand core.

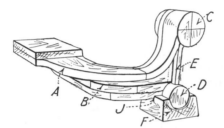

FIG. 173.—The pattern for the bracket.

Making the mold. Fill the *cope* with sand and bed the pattern in and roughly form the shape of the parting upon which the drag is to be rammed. The impression of the top surface of the flange A and the semicircumference of the boss C is taken by the sand of the cope. This is termed making a *temporary or false cope*. It is used only in forming the parting, and therefore is not a part of the finished mold.

Figure 174 illustrates the drag in course of making. The ramming of the sand has reached the top of the core-print F. The sand has been struck off level with the top of the print, and the print drawn out. The *core-print* with the attached boss D is shown to the right of its depression left in the sand.

The *dry sand core G*, which forms one half of the cylindrical surface of the boss and a small portion of the rib, is shown *directly above the depression it is to enter.*

Following the setting of the core G, the ramming of the drag is carried to completion. It is then rolled over in the usual way, the false cope removed and the parting for the permanent cope prepared.

Figure 175 illustrates the various parts of the pattern which have been dressed to shape and are ready to be attached together.

The height of the rib B is built up by *laminated construction*. This form of construction eliminates cross grain wood, and is used whenever the *maximum strength* of a thin curved member is required.

The laminated rib in course of building is shown in Fig. 176. The thickness of the layers is unimportant; the strength of

Fig. 174.—The mold ready to receive the cover-core *G*.

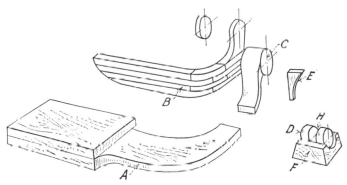

Fig. 175.—The members of the pattern shaped and ready to be attached together.

the construction is proportional to the number of layers. The width of the layers is to be determined from the layout of the rib.

The core-print *F*, Fig. 175 consists of a block containing a semicylindrical cavity. Attached within the cavity is the

boss *D*.   Instead of cutting out the rib *B*, Fig. 173 to conform
to the circumference of the boss *D*, the boss is cut out as
at *H*, Fig. 175.   This arrangement allows the boss to slip

FIG. 176.—Method of building up the rib.

FIG. 177.—Core-box used in connection with the pattern for the bracket.

down over the rib, and is the means of locating the core-print
in its proper place.   A dowel-pin holds the core-print in its
correct position.

The rib is cut out as at *J*, Fig. 173 to allow the faces of the
core-print to be in the same plane with the axis of boss *D*.
A piece corresponding in shape to that cut from the rib as
at *J*, is placed in the core-box as at *K*, Fig. 177.

Ordinarily the practice as previously described is to
separate the frame from the bottom-board of a core-box.

In case of the core-box shown in Fig. 177 this is unnecessary, as the *slant* upon the walls of the cavity and the form
of the parts attached to the bottom-board, will permit the
box to leave the core without interference.

PATTERN 24

GEAR-CASE

Features presented:
Coring out a casting in order to strengthen a pattern
Core-box construction
Figure 178 is the drawing of a brass gear-case

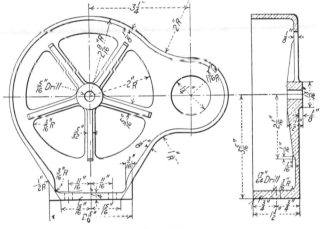

FIG. 178.

Interior and exterior surfaces of castings whose pattern would easily deliver its impression in the sand, are frequently formed by dry sand cores *for the sake of the added strength* given the pattern.

If the pattern for the gear-case shown were made to deliver the impression of its interior surfaces, it would be so *fragile* that it would not withstand foundry usage.

Figure 179 illustrates how the pattern is made solid, the interior of the casting being formed by a dry sand core.

11   161

The depth of the pattern is made up of three thicknesses of material. Thickness *A* represents the core-print, which is made ¼ inch; *B*, the depth of the interior of the casting; and *C*, the web thickness.

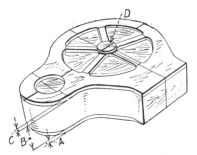

Fɪɢ. 179.—The pattern for the gear case.

The spider *D* *is not cut out* of the web thickness, but made independent and then attached.

Figure 180 illustrates the core-box. It consists of a frame and bottom-board of the usual construction. The frame is

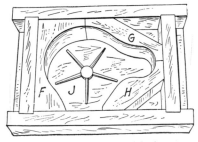

Fɪɢ. 180.—The core-box used in connection with the pattern for the gear case

filled in with the necessary loose material, *F*, *G* and *H*, to produce the required shape of the core cavity. The pieces *F*, *G* and *H* are fitted into place, then the shape of the core cavity *laid out.*

The pieces are dropped into place, the ramming in of the sand forcing them back into their correct position. The boss and the ribs indicated by *J*, are attached to the bottom-board.

This construction is particularly adapted to shaping cores that have projections occurring upon the walls of the core cavity at a point *above the bottom-board.*

The location of the pieces in their relation to the frame is to be *plainly indicated.* The use of the loose pieces do not permit the use of fillets, therefore, the box is to indicate where *filleted corners of the casting is required. Refer to the information on the marking of loose pattern parts given with pattern 18, page 142.*

In the case of right- and left-hand cores of greater proportions, this type of box is used to advantage in the saving of *lime and material,* as the frame and the bottom-board may be employed in the making of both cores.

A core-box of this type requires no draft and little if any rapping to remove it from the core.

QUESTIONS

1. What is understood by the term loose piece as applied to a pattern?

2. What means are employed in attaching loose pieces?

3. When a loose piece is to be taken out through a narrow cavity of mold, how should it be attached?

4. What is a loose dowel?

5. What is understood by the term tie-piece as applied to a pattern?

6. What is understood by the term stop off as applied to a mold?

7. How should a pattern indicate that the operation of stopping off is to be performed?

8. Describe the cornering tool.

9. When is a tail core-print used?

10. Describe how that portion of a pattern supporting a loose piece attached with dowel pins is rammed up.

11. Explain the use of a cake or covering core.

12. What is the purpose of making a false cope?

13. Define the term laminated construction as applied to pattern work.

14. What pattern features were presented by the hopper pattern?

15. What is the contraction allowance for brass?

16. What pattern feature was presented by the gear case pattern?

17. What was learned from the core-box for the gear case?

PART II
LATHE WORK

PATTERN TURNING

Wood turning, as practiced in pattern-making, differs from what might be termed ornamental or spindle turning, in that the *flat-chisel* takes the place of the gouge and skew-chisel as employed in the latter. The waste material is removed by a *scraping operation* instead of a cutting operation.

In pattern turning, the *gouge* is used principally for *roughing down* the surfaces preparatory to scraping, while the skew-chisel is used as a *cut off tool*.

The reason for using the scraping method in pattern work is because a *high degree of accuracy* is required. This is more easily obtained by the use of these tools.

Fig. 181.—Motor head-block speed lathe.

The work is divided into two classes; namely, between center turning and face-plate turning.

Between center turning is the term applied to that class of work which permits of the waste material being removed while the work is being revolved between the two centers of the lathe.

Face-plate turning is the term applied to that class of work whose shape required that it be turned while secured to a face-plate. The face-plate is attached to the spindle of the lathe.

The way a piece of material is mounted in the lathe for turning usually depends upon its proportions. If the length is greater than the diameter, it is usually turned *between centers*. If the length is less than the diameter, it is secured to a face-plate.

To operate any machine tool intelligently and safely, the beginner should be thoroughly familiar with its *operation and control*. He should study its construction and mechanism, and familiarize himself with the names of its component parts.

Figure 181 illustrates a motor head-block speed lathe. Lathes are classified as to their size by the maximum diameter in inches of work which may be revolved over the ways.

The speed lathe as shown may be said to comprise four essential features, the bed, the headstock, the tailstock and the tool rest mechanism.

The bed. The bed forms the main casting of the lathe and is carried upon two supports, one at each end of the bed.

A slot or inside ways furnish a permanent seat for the *headstock* and a perfect aligned seat for any desired position of the *tailstock*.

The tool-rest. The tool rest is made up of several pieces. Its function is to provide a rest or support for the turning tools. A clamping arrangement permits the rest to be set and clamped in any desired position in front of the work.

EXERCISE 6

Features presented:
Centering rectangular stock
Mounting material between the centers of lathe
Setting the tool-rest
The turning-gouge
Grinding and whetting turning tools
Outside-calipers
Establishing the diameter of a cylinder
The parting-tool
The flat-chisel
Application of the dividers
The skew-chisel
Figure 182 is the drawing of a cylinder.

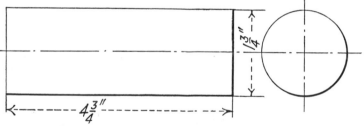

Fig. 182.—Drawing of the cylinder to be turned.

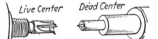

Fig. 183.—The lathe centers.

The length of the cylinder is greater than the diameter, therefore it will be turned between the centers of the lathe.

Figure 183 illustrates and gives the names of the lathe centers.

Stock required: 2 × 2 × 6¼ inches

ORDER OF OPERATIONS

1. Center the material by drawing diagonals across each end. The *center points* are located at the intersections of the diagonals.

A hammer should never be used for *driving* in the *live-center*, for it will likely *upset* the end of the center, and prevent it from properly *fitting the spindle*. *Use a mallet*. The dead-center, as it is called, because it does not revolve, need not be driven in. It may be forced in by the forward movement of the tail-stock spindle. Exert enough pressure on the center to force it into the wood sufficiently to produce a good impression; then withdraw the center just enough to allow the work to *revolve easily*. A drop of oil or a little soap, placed in the dead-center, will prevent *squeaking*.

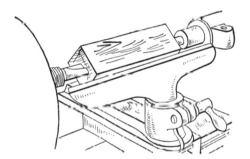

Fig. 184.—Material mounted between the centers of a lathe.

Figure 184 illustrates the material mounted between the centers of the lathe.

The tool supporting edge of the tool-rest should be set about ⅛ *inch below* the axis of rotation, and ⅜ *inch in front of the work and parallel to* it. As the waste is turned off, the tool-rest is moved forward, so as to maintain the support of the tool near the work. A disregard *for the resetting of the tool-rest may result in a broken tool*.

The Turning-gouge.—The turning-gouge is used for roughing down surfaces preparatory to scraping.

2. With the *gouge,* rough down the material.

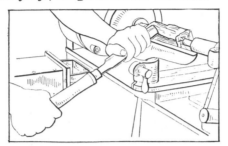

FIG. 185.—Roughing down the material with a gouge.

Figure 185 illustrates how the gouge is held. The face of the gouge should always be *tipped in the direction* in which the gouge is being moved, otherwise it is apt to catch and be *drawn into the work.*

Hold the gouge *firmly down* on the tool-rest. Begin with a light cut at the live-center end. Move the gouge along the tool-rest until a cut has been taken throughout the length of the material. Reverse the position of the gouge and begin the cut from the opposite end. Repeat the operation until a cylinder of the greatest possible diameter has been produced.

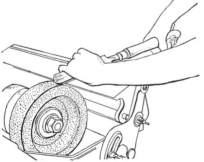

FIG. 186.—Grinding a turning-gouge.

When the repeated whetting of a tool has rounded the cutting edge to the extent that it does not cut *easily or smoothly* the tool should be *ground.* A turning-gouge is shown being ground in Fig. 186.

Don't use a dry stone.

Don't exert enough pressure on a tool when grinding to cause heating of the edge to the extent of *drawing the temper.*

Don't hold a tool in one place, for a groove in the stone will likely result.

The gouge is whetted as shown in Fig. 187. As the *slip* is given an elliptical movement, the gouge is rocked, that the entire length of the edge may be sharpened. The rounded edge of the slip is then applied to the concave surface. It is given a lengthwise movement. Repeat the above operations until a sharp edge has been produced.

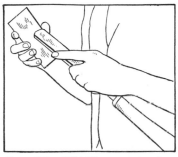

FIG. 187.—Whetting a turning-gouge with a slip-stone.

Calipers.—Calipers are used by the pattern-maker for measuring and transferring the distances between two surfaces and to verify the diameter of turned work.

Figure 188 shows how a dimension is taken from a rule with outside calipers of the firm joint type. This type of calipers has no means of close adjustment. They are first set to the approximate distance, then the final adjustment made by *tapping* the leg lightly in the direction required.

Calipers should be so held that they may be *guided by a sensitive touch.*

Calipering *revolving work* should be carefully done, for *injury* is likely to result should the calipers catch

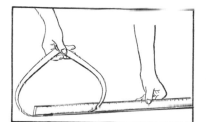

FIG. 188.—Taking a dimension from a rule with the outside calipers.

in the material. If forced against the work, one contact of the calipers will likely be drawn over by the friction of the revolving surface, *causing the measurement taken to be inaccurate and misleading.*

The Parting-tool.—The parting-tool is used for turning narrow recesses and grooves.

3. Establish with the *parting-tool* and the aid of the calipers, as shown in Fig. 189, the diameter of the cylinder. This operation consists of turning a series of narrow grooves about 1 inch apart, throughout the length of the stock. The

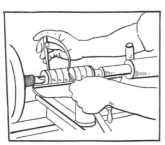

FIG. 189.—Establishing with the parting-tool and aid of the calipers the diameter of the cylinder.

FIG. 190.—Grinding a parting-tool.

lower angle of the cutting edge of the parting tool is kept approximately *tangent* to the surface being turned. To maintain this position as the work is reduced in diameter, the handle end of the tool is *raised,* causing the cutting edge to follow the diminishing surface.

FIG. 191.—Whetting a parting-tool.

The parting-tool is shown being ground in Fig. 190; it is shown being whetted in Fig. 191. The included angle of point should be about 25 *degrees.*

The Flat-chisel.—The flat-chisel is used for turning flat or convex surfaces.

4. Turn off the waste between the grooves and complete the cylindrical surface with a flat-chisel, as shown in Fig. 192.

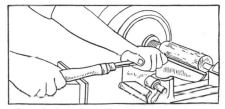

FIG. 192.—Completing the cylindrical surface with a flat chisel.

The chisel should lie *flat* upon the tool-rest, the face of the chisel up.

The flat-chisel is ground and whetted in the same manner as a plane-bit.

5. Lay off the length of the cylinder.

Figure 193 shows how the *dividers* are used to transfer the length dimension from the rule to the work. Set the tool-rest *close up to the work*. Hold both points of the dividers down upon the tool-rest, *then lightly push them against the revolving surface.*

Divide the amount of waste in the length of work *between each end, so that the depression made by either center shall not appear in the finished cylinder.*

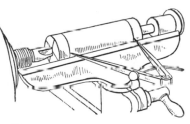

FIG. 193.—Transfering from the rule to the work with the dividers, the length dimension of the cylinder.

The Skew-chisel.—T h e skew-chisel is used for cutting work to length.

6. Turn or cut the cylinder to length with the *skew-chisel* as shown in Fig. 194.

Figure 195 illustrates the skew-chisel being ground. The ground surfaces are whetted in the same manner as the ground surface of a flat-chisel.

The ground surface of the skew-chisel which is toward the work, is to *parallel the end surface* of the cylinder.   *To the beginner, this will be found the most difficult operation to perform.*

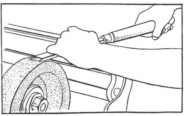

Fig. 194.—Cutting the cylinder to   Fig. 195—Grinding a skew-chisel.
length with a skew-chisel.

If the cutting edge of the skew-chisel is *tipped toward the work, it will likely catch, and be carried over onto the cylindrical surface.*

Turn the end surfaces of the cylinder at *right angles to its axis.*   Test the surface with one of the corner edges of tool while performing this operation.   As in the use of the parting-tool, so the handle of the skew-chisel is *raised* as the cut is carried toward the axis of the cylinder.

Deep cuts will cause *excessive friction,* which is likely to *impair* the temper of the tool.

The first cut is made about ½ *inch* beyond the length of the cylinder.   By a *series of light cuts, increasing the depth*

Fig. 196.—The cylinder at the completion of the turning operation.

of each succeeding cut, the waste is removed until the end surface of the cylinder is turned.   Do not turn the end surfaces, farther toward the axial line than a ½-inch diameter.   The end of the cylinder toward the *dead-center* should be turned first; the turning of the live-center end completes the lathe work.

The work is to appear at the completion of the turning operation, as shown in Fig. 196.

7. Saw off the waste material and finish the end surfaces with a paring-chisel.

If for any reason work is to be removed from the lathe before completion, the position of the *live-center should be marked,* in order that the work may be replaced in the same position.

Reminders

Check yourself up on safety practices. Get the *"safety first habit."*

When *"safety first"* causes a delay, it is well worth it and time well spent.

Form the habit of never standing in line with swiftly revolving parts, such as saws, emery wheels and work secured to face plates.

A ring may be ornamental, but a *dangerous* thing to wear when operating a lathe.

Never *hit* the edge of a tempered tool, or hit a file with a hammer; good *eye-sight* is a wonderful blessing.

EXERCISE 7

Features presented:
  Taper turning
  Mounting work for taper turning
  Centering cylindrical stock
  Testing a conical surface
  Sandpapering a revolving surface

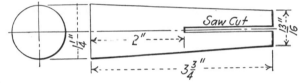

FIG. 197.—Drawing of the sandpapering roll.

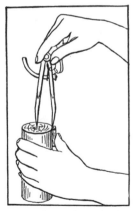

FIG. 198.—Centering cylindrical
stock with the dividers.

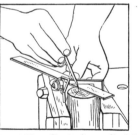

FIG. 199.—Centering cylindrical
stock with a center-square.

Figure 197 is the drawing of a tapered sandpapering roll.
The saw cut made along the axis of the roll is for the purpose
of securing the sandpaper.

176

It is a little more difficult to turn an object of this general form than to turn a cylindrical object.

The usual procedure in turning a tapered object of this kind is to *establish at the required distance the two end diameters.* The waste material is then turned off until a conical surface has been produced.

Stock required: 1½ × 1½ × 5 inches

If desired, the roll may be turned from the cylinder exercise.

Cylindrical stock is centered by scribing arcs Fig. 198 from three different points upon the circumference. The lathe centers locate at the intersection of the arcs.

Center-square.—A blade so arranged with a square as to have one edge of the blade divide the angle of the square equally. To center cylindrical stock, Fig. 199, hold both limbs of the head *firmly* against the work and with a *scriber* draw lines at about right angles.

ORDER OF OPERATIONS

1. Center and mount stock as for a cylinder.

2. As the length of the roll is given parallel to its axis, turn a cylinder of about 1⅜ inches diameter and lay off the length of the roll upon it.

FIG. 200.—The work with the length dimension established.

3. Establish the length by *partially turning* the end surfaces as at A, Fig. 200.

4. Establish the large diameter of the roll by turning a *cylindrical surface as at B,* Fig. 201, whose diameter is equal to this dimension.

5. Establish the small diameter of the roll by turning a *cylindrical surface as at C,* Fig. 201. The diameter C is turned in the *waste* material beyond the *limit* of the tapered surface.

12

Whenever possible, it is a good practice to arrange the material for tapered work so that the *small end* of the object shall be toward the *dead-center.* This position will not only tend to *eliminate vibration* but will permit the small end to be *more closely turned* to the axial line.

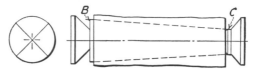

Fig. 201.—The work with the large and the small diameters of the roll established.

6. Turn the roll to the required taper, as shown in broken lines. As the turning of the conical surface progresses, its accuracy is *tested* with a straight-edge. *Do not test* the surface while the lathe is in *motion.* If the edge of the straight-edge is *blackened with lead,* the lead will be transferred to the *high places,* indicating where further turning is required.

Fig. 202.—The roll at the completion of the turning operation.

7. Turn the end surfaces *A*, Fig. 202, farther toward the axial line (about ⅜-inch diameter). Always turn the end which is toward the *dead-center first,* then complete the lathe work by turning the live-center end. If this order of turning the end surfaces is reversed, the small neck that must *drive the work, may be broken off when turning the dead-center end.*

Sandpapering.—The sandpapering of work is done with a medium fine grade of paper (No. 0).

A strip of sandpaper about 1 inch wide and 3 inches long is used. Grip the ends of the strip between the thumb and the first finger of each hand. As the sandpaper is pressed against the surface of the roll and made to conform to it, pass the paper back and forth in the direction of the length of the roll.

8. Scribe a line around the roll, to establish the length of the saw cut. The line along which the saw cut is made is

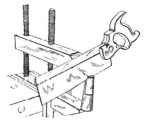

Fig. 203.—Making the saw-cut in the roll with a back-saw.

drawn by placing the tool rest against the roll and scribing a pencil line along the top of the rest. Figure 202 illustrates the roll as it will appear when ready to be removed from the lathe.

9. Remove the work from the lathe and complete the end surfaces as in the case of the cylinder.

10. Secure the roll in a hand-screw as shown in Fig. 203 and make the saw cut with a back-saw.

EXERCISE 8

Features presented:

Turning core-prints

Turning a number of similarly shaped objects from one
piece of material

Figure 204 is the drawing of a cope and drag core-print.

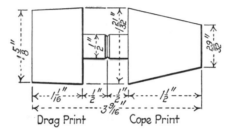

Fig. 204.—Drawing of the core-prints to be turned.

When a number of core-prints or similar objects are wanted,
several may be turned from the same piece of material. This
method not only results in the saving of time, but in eliminat-
ing the waste that would be cut from each end of the objects if
turned separately.

Stock required: 2 × 2 × 5 inches

ORDER OF OPERATIONS

1. Mount the material.

2. Turn a cylinder whose diameter equals the *greatest
diameter* of the core-prints.

3. Lay off the over-all lengths of the prints.

4. From the line nearest the dead-center end of the work,
lay off the length of the tapered or cope print. Lay off from
the line nearest the live-center end, the length of the drag
print.

5. Establish these dimensions by *partially turning* the end surfaces of the prints as at *A*, Fig. 205.

6. Turn the core-prints to *required shape* as indicated by the *broken lines*.

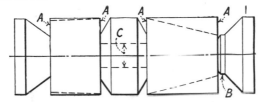

FIG. 205.—The work with the length dimensions established.

7. Turn the dowel *C* and complete the adjacent end surfaces of the prints.

8. Turn the end surfaces farther toward the axial line. The work at the completion of the turning operation will appear as shown in Fig. 206.

9. Sandpaper and shellac the work.

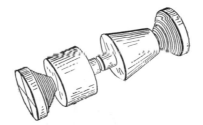

FIG. 206.—The core-prints at the completion of the turning operation.

Refer to instruction on shellacking given with Pattern 1, page 46.

Do not sandpaper or shellac the dowel or the adjacent end surfaces of the prints.

10. When the shellac has *thoroughly dried*, remount the work in the lathe and sandpaper the shellacked surfaces.

A very fine grade of sandpaper should be used for sandpapering a revolving shellacked surface.

Complete the end surfaces of the prints as instructed, then shellac.

FACE-PLATE TURNING

Material is usually mounted in the lathe for face-plate turning by one of three methods.

The Screw-plate.—The screw-plate *A* or *B*, Fig. 207, is used when the work is comparatively small.   The length of the *screw*

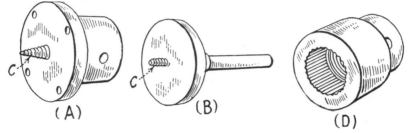

(A)   (B)   (D)

FIG. 207.—Screw plates or chucks.   Cup chuck.

C is determined by the diameter and the thickness of the object to be turned.   No. 14, 16 or 18 is the screw generally used for a screw plate.

The Cup Chuck.—The cup chuck *D* is used when the grain of wood lies parallel to the axis of rotation and when it is desired to have the *end free*, in order that this surface may be

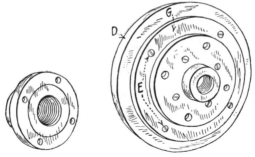

FIG. 208.—Face plates.

recessed or turned to the *axial line*.   The material is secured by driving it into the chuck.

Face-plates.—Face-plates of the general type shown in Fig. 208 are used when the material exceeds 6 inches in diameter, or when the center screw *C*, Fig. 207, would interfere with the turning operation at or near the center of rotation.

Face-plates vary in diameter from 3 inches up. Their selection depends upon the size and nature of the work. *The screws securing the material to a face-plate should be placed at as great a distance from the center of rotation as the work will permit.*

The material is secured by two or more screws as the case may require. They are inserted through holes in the flange of the face-plate.

Due to the clearance between the thread in the face-plate and the thread on the spindle, the face-plate will not always *line up when remounted.*

Whenever it is *necessary* to have the axis of the pattern at *right angles* to the face toward the face plate, an intermediate thickness or facing of wood *G*, Fig. 208, should be secured to the face-plate and then carefully trued up to receive the pattern material *D*.

If the diameter of the material *D* will not permit of the locating of the screws *E* outside the limit of the face-plate as shown, the screws securing the facing *G* are withdrawn and screws inserted which are long enough to pass through the facing and enter the work. To prevent the displacement of the facing *G*, each screw as it is withdrawn is replaced by a longer screw before withdrawing another screw.

Screw holes left by the screws used to secure work to a face-plate, *are not to be relied* upon to bring the work back to its original setting.

Unfinished work should never be removed from a face-plate unless provision has been made for its correct replacement.

QUESTIONS

1. What is understood by the expression between center turning?

2. What is understood by the expression face-plate turning?

3. What usually determines the way a piece of work is to be mounted in the lathe?

4. What is meant by dead-center?

5. What is meant by live-center?

6. How is rectangular stock usually centered?

7. Why should a hammer never be used to drive the live center into the material?

8. What makes the dead-center become heated, causing it to squeak?

9. How may the squeaking be stopped?

10. How should the tool-rest be set in its relation to the work to be turned?

11. Why should the rest be kept near the surface being turned?

12. For what purpose is the turning-gouge principally used?

13. Why should the face of the gouge be tipped in the direction the cut is being made?

14. For what purpose are calipers used?

15. How is the final adjustment made with calipers of the firm joint type?

16. Why should calipering revolving work be carefully done?

17. For what purpose is the parting-tool principally used?

18. What position should the lower angle of the cutting edge of the parting-tool bear to the surface being turned?

19. For what purpose is the skew-chisel principally used?

20. What position should the ground surface of the chisel which is toward the surface being turned, bear to this surface?

21. What portion of a skew-chisel does the cutting?

22. Why should the finishing of the end of the work toward the dead-center precede the finishing of the live-center end?

23. How is a conical surface tested?

24. Describe the construction of the center-square and explain its use.

25. Why is it good practice to arrange the material so that the small end of a tapered object will be toward the dead-center?

26. What is the advantage in turning a number of similar shaped objects from the same piece of material?

27. How is the taper of a conical shaped roll established?

PATTERN 25

BASE

Features presented:
Face-plate turning
Preparing and mounting material upon a face-plate
Application of the dividers
The diamond-point tool
The round-nose tool
Figure 209 is the drawing of a cast iron base.

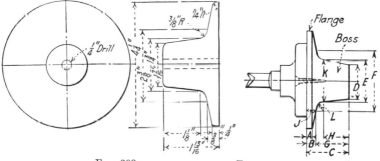

FIG. 209.   FIG. 210.—Reference diagram

The casting consists of a circular flange of diminishing thickness supporting a tapered boss.

A fillet connects the conical surfaces of the boss with the conical surface of the back of the flange.

Figure 210 is used for reference; letters designate the various dimensions of the pattern.

Material to be mounted upon a face-plate is sawed in the form of a disc. The disc is to be ⅜ *inch greater in diameter than the required pattern, and* ⅛ *inch greater in thickness.*

The surface of the material which is placed against the face-plate is to be *planed true.*

185

For the patterns to follow, this operation will be referred to as "*prepare and mount the material.*"

Stock required: $1^{15}\!/_{16} \times 4^{3}\!/_{4} \times 4^{3}\!/_{4}$ inches

ORDER OF OPERATIONS

Figure 211 shows the material mounted upon a screw-plate. Sufficient accuracy will be obtained by mounting the work as shown. One-quarter of the material has been removed in order to expose the screw. The screw used in this case is No. 14. *It enters the wood about 1 inch.*

1. Reduce the material to the *greatest* given diameter of the pattern.

The roughing down operation is to be done with a *flat-chisel*. *Do not make a cut* with the full width of the chisel, but remove the waste by making cuts of $\frac{1}{8}$ *inch width.* Any attempt

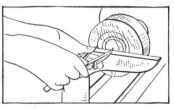

FIG. 211.—The material mounted upon a screw-plate.

FIG. 212.—Scribing circumferences of the pattern upon the face of the material.

to take a *heavy cut* with the full width of the chisel, or with a *dull chisel*, will likely result in *stripping the material from the screw.* The turning of end grain wood destroys the cutting edge of a tool very quickly and necessitates frequent whetting.

2. Upon the circumference turned, scribe with the dividers the dimensions of the patterns represented by the letters *A*, *B* and *C*, Fig. 210.

3. Reduce the material to the dimension represented by *C*. To perform this operation, the tool-rest is set at right angles

to the axis of rotation of the lathe, or *in front of the material.* Set the tool-rest so that the tool will be supported near the surface being turned.

4. Revolve the work and locate with pencil the center of rotation. From this point scribe with the dividers, as illustrated in Fig. 212, circumferences the diameters of which are represented by *D*, *E* and *F*.

5. Establish the thickness of flange at *J* by turning a cylinder whose diameter is represented by *F* and length by *G*.

6. Turn the flange to thickness. The *diamond-point* tool is best suited for this operation.

Fig. 213.—Grinding a diamond-point tool.

Fig. 214.—Whetting a round-nose tool.

The Diamond-point.—The diamond-point has *two cutting edges* inclined to one another and meeting at an acute angle. It is used for turning surfaces which are not *accessible to,* or cannot be conveniently turned with a flat-chisel. The grinding of a diamond-point is shown in Fig. 213.

7. Establish the large diameter of the boss as at *K* by turning a cylinder whose diameter is represented by *E* and length by *H*.

8. Turn the conical surface of the boss.

9. Turn the fillet *L*. The *round-nose tool* is used for this operation.

The Round-nose.—The round-nose tool has the cutting edge curved. It is used for turning *concave surfaces.*

The whetting of a round-nose tool is illustrated in Fig. 214. The tool is *rocked* as it is pushed forward over the surface of the stone. The tool is ground in the same manner as the turning-gouge. The curve of the cutting edge depends somewhat upon the width of the blade.

10. Turn the rounded corner of the flange. Rounded corners are to be turned with the flat-chisel or diamond-point tool.

If the drawing shows a rounded corner, and it is not dimensioned, *assume that a $\frac{1}{16}$-inch radius is required.* If a fillet is not dimensioned, assume, on small machine parts, that a $\frac{1}{8}$-*inch radius is required.*

11. Sandpaper, then shellac the pattern. When the shellac has thoroughly dried, sandpaper the work in the lathe.

12. Detach from the face-plate and close with a wooden plug, the hole in the face of the flange made by the screw; then sandpaper and shellac this surface of the pattern.

PATTERN 26

COLLAR

Features presented:
  Securing material to a face-plate
  Turning an interior surface or wall of a hole
  Inside calipers
  Sandpapering revolving interior surfaces.
Figure 215 is the drawing of a cast iron collar.

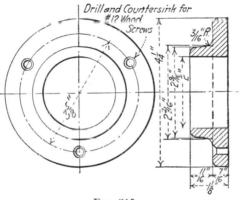

Fig. 215.

The casting consists of a circular flange from which projects a ring.

Three holes appear in the flange. The drawing specifies they are to be drilled and countersunk for No. 12 wood screws.

Countersinking is the conical enlargement of the end of a hole. This is a machine shop operation and does not affect the pattern.

It will be readily seen that the material for the pattern cannot be mounted upon a screw-plate, as the screw would

189

interfere with the *turning out of the hole*. It is therefore mounted upon a face-plate as clearly shown in Fig. 216.

To clearly illustrate the method of attaching the work, a section of the material and facing is shown removed.

Attention is called to the manner of separating the pattern material from the face-plate by a facing of wood as indicated

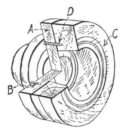

FIG. 216.—The work at the completion of the hole.

by *A*. This is done for two reasons; *first*, to assure a *true* running surface upon which to mount the work, and *second*, to allow the wall of the hole to be turned to completion, without the edge of the turning tool coming in *contact* with the metal face-plate.

The face-plate contains four screw holes. Screws are inserted, at *B*, through the holes which are diametrically opposite. *They secure the facing A*.

The material *C* for the pattern is secured by the screws *D*, which pass through the face plate and the facing *A*.

To locate the face-plate upon the material, scribe a circumference which is the diameter of the face-plate.

Figure 217 is used for reference in dimensioning the pattern.

Stock required: $1\frac{1}{4} \times 4\frac{5}{8} \times 4\frac{5}{8}$ inches. Pattern

$\frac{3}{4} \times 4\frac{5}{8} \times 4\frac{5}{8}$ inches. Facing

ORDER OF OPERATIONS

1. Prepare and mount the material upon a face plate. *Be careful* that the portion of the screws *D*, entering the material, does not exceed the thickness of the flange, and, as a result, *interfere* with the turning of this member.

2. Turn the material to the *greatest diameter* of pattern, then upon its circumference scribe the dimensions represented by *B* and *C*, Fig. 217.

3. Turn to dimension *C*.

4. Upon the face of the material scribe the circumferences represented by *D*, *E*, *F* and *G*.

Diameter *G* is the large diameter of the ring portion *plus twice the radius J*.

A form will be less likely to split if the inside is turned first, and then the outside is turned.

The *diamond-point tool* is used for turning the interior surface. Failure to keep the tool *sharp* or *firmly* held down upon the tool rest will result in an *inaccurate surface*.

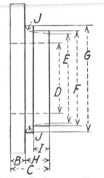

FIG. 217.—Reference diagram.

5. At the center of rotation begin operations with the point of the tool taking *light cuts* and working toward the circumference, until a hole slightly less than the given diameter *D* has been turned through the material. With the aid of the inside calipers turn the hole to the required diameter.

Inside Calipers.—Inside calipers are chiefly used for transferring dimensions to interior surfaces.

Warning: *Never attempt to use the inside calipers while the lathe is in motion.*

Figure 218 shows the correct way of taking a dimension from the rule with the inside calipers of the spring type.

Do not fail to provide draft upon the wall of the hole.

6. Turn the flange to thickness B.   The thickness of the flange is formed by turning a cylinder whose diameter is represented by G, and length by H.

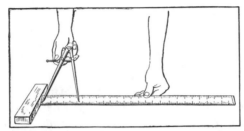

Fig. 218.—Taking a dimension from a rule with the inside calipers.

7. Turn a cylinder whose diameter is represented by F and length by I.

8. Turn the ring to required shape.

9. Turn the fillet J and round the corner of the flange and the ring.

To sandpaper the interior surface of the pattern, fold a piece of sandpaper to about ½ inch width and hold it under the first or second finger.

Finish the pattern.

PATTERN 27

COVER

Features presented:

Rechucking a piece of work

Determining the surface to be turned first

Separating a piece of work from the face-plate with a turning tool

Right and left-hand side-tools

Securing a piece of work to a false chuck by friction

Chalking or moistening contacting surfaces to obtain additional adherence

Application of the dividers

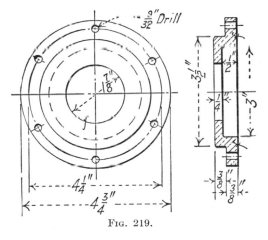

Fig. 219.

Figure 219 is the drawing of a brass cover.

The casting consists of a circular flange supporting a web of ¼ inch thickness. A 1⅞-inch finished hole is required in the web.

Whenever a green sand core forming a hole in a casting is delivered by the pattern, and the hole is required to be finished, the *finish allowance* is to be *increased* by the amount of *draft* given the walls of the hole.

The face of the flange is required to be finished; therefore it will be molded in the drag. *Refer to the information on the requirements of a casting determining the molding position of the pattern given with Pattern 4, page 59.*

Rechucking.—When all surfaces of a pattern are to be turned to dimension, it involves an operation known as *rechucking*. This means that at the completion of the turning of one face of the pattern, the work is detached from the face-plate and *reversed*. This allows the surface which was against the face-plate to be turned. The face of the work to be turned first will usually depend upon the shape of the pattern.

Material required: $^{15}\!\!/_{16} \times 5\frac{1}{8} \times 5\frac{1}{8}$ inches.   Pattern
 $\frac{7}{8} \times 4\frac{1}{8} \times 4\frac{1}{8}$ inches.   Chuck

ORDER OF OPERATIONS

1. Prepare and mount the material upon a *screw-plate*.
2. True up the face of the material, then turn to the greatest diameter of the pattern.

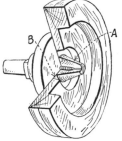

FIG. 220.—The work at the completion of the first turning operation.

The *recessed* face of the pattern will be turned first, because the circular wall of the recess affords the best means of centering and securing the work to the chuck. *Attention* is called to this feature, because the general practice is to *turn first that face of an object* which affords the most accurate and secure way of *rechucking*.

3. Scribe upon the face of the material a circumference whose diameter is that of the recess. Then proceed to turn out this depression to the shape shown in Fig. 220. The bottom surface of the recess is not carried to the center of rotation, but stock is allowed to remain about the screw at *A*.

4. Sandpaper and apply one coat of shellac to this face of the work.

The Side-tool, Fig. 221.—The side-tool is a *modified diamond-point tool.* It is used to turn the walls of small holes or openings which are not accessible to the wider blade of the

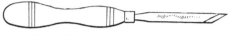

FIG. 221.—A right-hand side-tool.

diamond-point. The included angle of the point should be about 20 *degrees.* Side-tools are usually made in pairs, *right-hand and left-hand.*

5. Separate the work from the face-plate with a *side-tool* by turning a groove of 1⅝ inches or less diameter, *to within ¹⁄₁₆* inch of the face-plate, as at *B.* The work is then removed from the plate and the separation completed with the *point of a knife.*

The chucking material or false chuck as indicated by *C,* Fig. 222, is sawed about 3⅞ inches in diameter (thickness unimportant) and attached to a *screw-plate* as shown.

6. Prepare and mount the chucking material, then turn upon its face the projection indicated by *D.* Make projection *D* about ¼ inch. This projection is to enter the recess as shown.

As the work is secured to the chuck by *friction,* it is very important that a *close fit* be made between the circumference of the projection *D* and the wall of the recess. To obtain a *true setting,* the surfaces of the chuck and of the work *must come in contact, as at E.* Additional adherence may be obtained

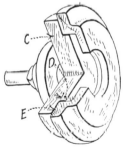

FIG. 222.—The work rechucked and the turning operation completed.

by *chalking,* or by very slightly *moistening* the circumference of the projection *D.*

7. Scribe upon the circumference of the material the thickness of the flange and the over-all thickness of the pattern. Then turn the material to the latter dimension.

8. Scribe upon the face of the material circumferences which represent the diameter of the hole and the diameter of the web.

Whenever laying out, or scribing the circumferenc of a hole the wall of which is required to be finished; keep in mind, that the finish allowance is to be *subtracted* from the radius of the hole.

Figure 223 illustrates how a circumference may be scribed with a pair of dividers upon a revolving surface, when the

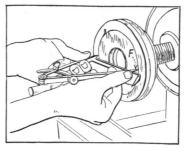

Fig. 223.—Scribing a circle upon a revolving surface, when the center of rotation of the surface has been destroyed.

center of rotation of the surface has been *destroyed or is inaccessible.* The dividers are set to the *required diameter of the circle.* Point *F* of the dividers does not *touch* the surface of the work, but is used to locate and verify the dimension.

In scribing a circle in this manner the tool rest is to be set about ⅛ inch away from the surface of the work.

9. Complete the turning operation and finish the pattern in the usual way.

PATTERN 28

CYLINDER-HEAD

Features presented:
Application of templets
Laying out templets
Figure 224 is the drawing of a cast iron cylinder-head.

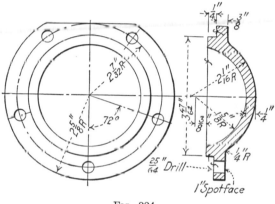

FIG. 224.

The casting consists of a circular flange supporting a spherical shell.

Surfaces of circular patterns are very often of such form or cross-section that *templets* are needed to test the correctness of their outline as the material is reduced to shape. In order to turn the *spherical* surface of the shell portion of the cylinder-head pattern, a reference is required, hence the use of templets.

The templets are made by laying out a cross-section of the pattern, as shown in Fig. 225, in the following way, upon a piece of material of about ⅛ inch thickness.

197

Scribe line *A*; gage line *B*; lay off distance *C*; scribe an arc using the radius *D*; lay off the distance *E*; scribe an arc using the radius *F*. Lay off the dimensions represented by *G* and *H* and scribe lines parallel to line *B*. The dimension represented by *G* is the amount of finish allowance to be provided upon this surface of the casting.

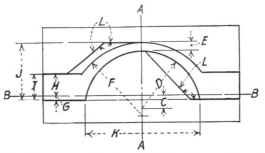

Fig. 225.—The shape of the templets laid out upon the material.

The testing surface of the templets need only represent a radial outline of the surface to be shaped; therefore, the templets are cut away or given clearance as at *L*.

Do not saw the templets to shape until the following dimensions represented by *I*, *J* and *K*, turning operation 3, have been transferred from the layout of the templets to the material.

Material required: $1\frac{3}{4} \times 5\frac{5}{8} \times 5\frac{5}{8}$ inches.   Pattern
$\qquad$ 1 $\times 5\frac{1}{2} \times 5\frac{1}{2}$ inches.   Chuck
$\qquad \frac{1}{8} \times 3\frac{1}{4} \times 6\frac{1}{4}$ inches.   Templets

ORDER OF OPERATIONS

1. Prepare the material and mount upon a face-plate as shown in Fig. 226.

2. True up the face and then turn to the greatest diameter of the pattern.

3. From the *face* of the work lay off and scribe upon the circumference, the dimensions represented by *I* and *J*. Scribe upon the face of the work the circumference represented by *K*.

Transfer these dimensions from the *layout of the templets.* Scribe upon the face of the work a circumference which is the diameter of the cylindrical projection upon the face of the flange.

4. Turn out the spherical depression. The *round-nose tool* is used for this operation.

As the turning of this surface nears completion, the lathe should be stopped frequently and the surface *tested* with the *templet.* This operation is repeated until the surface exactly corresponds to the *outline* of the templet and the *straight edge* of the templet comes in *contact* with the *face* of the work. When making a test, the face of the templet is to be in the

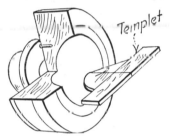

Fig. 226.—The work at the completion of the turning of the interior surface of the pattern.

same *plane* with the *center of rotation.* The outline of the templet will be *impaired* if testing is attempted while the work is in *motion.*

Figure 226 illustrates the work at the completion of this operation.

5. Turn the cylindrical projection on the face of the flange and finish this face of the pattern.

The lateral surface of the projection on the face of the flange is the means of centering and attaching the work to the chuck.

Like the preceding pattern the work is secured to the chuck by friction. When wood with the grain lying in a transverse direction to the axis of rotation is secured to a face-plate; the cutting qualities of the wood keep changing, due to the end and length grain.   Unless the cutting edge of the tool is kept as *sharp as possible,* the surface turned will be *inaccurate.*

6. Prepare and mount the chucking material and *rechuck* the work.

Figure 227 illustrates the pattern at the completion of the turning operation.

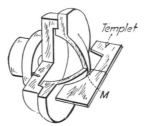

Fig. 227.—The work rechucked and the turning operation completed.

7. Reduce the work to the dimension represented by *J.*

8. Turn the flange to the dimension represented by *I* and then turn the spherical surface of the work.   At the completion of this operation, the *straight-edge* of the templet will be in *contact* with the *back* surface of the flange, and the center line *A* of the templet, coinciding at *M,* with the axis of the work.

9. Finish this surface of the work and then detach from chuck and complete the shape of the flange.

PATTERN 29

HAND-WHEEL

Features presented:
 Scribing a line upon an irregular surface
 Application of templets
 Securing rechucked work
 Application of the dividers
Figure 228 is the drawing of a cast iron hand-wheel.

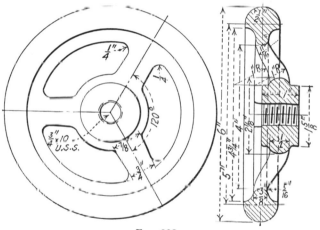

Fig. 228.

Hand-wheel patterns of small diameter and similar in form
to the one shown are usually turned from one piece of wood.
The shape of the arms is then laid out upon the web which
connects the hub with the rim, and later dressed to shape.

The templets required for the turning operation are made
by laying out upon a thin piece of material a radial section of

the pattern as shown in Fig. 229.   The outline of the pattern
is then cut away.

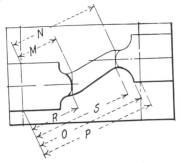

FIG. 229.—The shape of the templets laid out upon the material.

Stock required: $1\frac{5}{8} \times 6\frac{3}{8} \times 6\frac{3}{8}$ inches   Pattern
$1 \quad \times 5\frac{3}{8} \times 5\frac{3}{8}$ inches   Chuck
$\frac{1}{8} \times 3 \quad \times 4\frac{1}{4}$ inches   Templets

ORDER OF OPERATIONS

1. Prepare and mount the material upon a face-plate.

2. True up the face, then turn to the greatest diameter of the
pattern.   The *depressed* face of the pattern will be turned first.

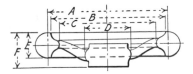

FIG. 230.—Reference diagram.

3. Scribe upon the face of the work the circumferences represented by A and B, Fig. 230.

4. From the *face* lay off and scribe upon the circumference
of the work the dimensions represented by E and F.

5. Turn a depression in the face down to the *surface of the
hub* and about $2\frac{1}{2}$ inches in diameter, then scribe upon it a
circumference which is the *diameter of the hub*.

6. Turn this face of the work to conform to its templet,
then sandpaper the surface.

7. Scribe the circumferences represented by C and D. To scribe these circumferences from the center of rotation, the distances represented by M and N, are taken from the templets, and used as the radii. The reason for these radii being used instead of the given radii is because the *center of rotation* upon the face of the hub is not in the *same plane* as the points upon the surface of the web where the circumferences are scribed.

8. Divide the circumference of the work into three equal parts; to secure the maximum strength, scribe the center line of

Fig. 231.—Scribing the center lines of the arms upon the depressed surface of the web.

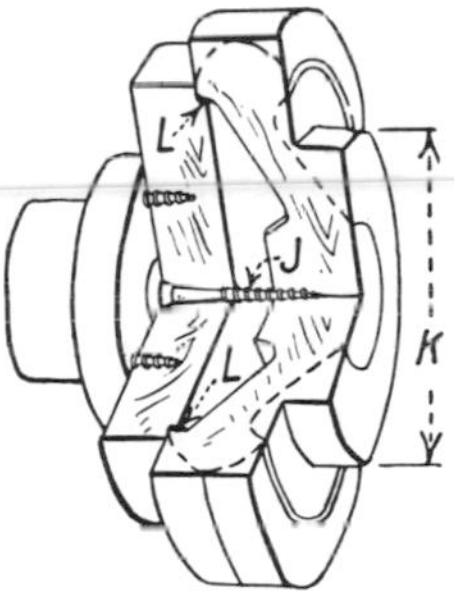

Fig. 232.—The work rechucked and in process of turning.

one arm in the direction of the grain of the wood. Square lines across the lateral surfaces as indicated by H, Fig. 231. From these division lines, scribe the center lines of the arms.

Figure 231 illustrates the method employed in scribing the center lines. The surface of block C is placed and held in a true plane with the required location of the line. The line is scribed with a narrow blade chisel while the face of the blade is held against the surface of the block as shown.

9. Lay out the shape of the arm upon heavy drawing-paper, then cut it to shape. This templet is then used to trace the outline of the arms upon the surface of the web.

10. Rechuck the work. The work is centered by a $\frac{1}{16}$ inch projection, turned upon the face of the chuck as at L, Fig. 232. The work is secured to the chuck with a screw located

at *J*. The diameter of the chuck cannot exceed 5 inches as it would interfere with the turning of the surface of the rim.

11. Turn the material to the thickness represented by *F*,

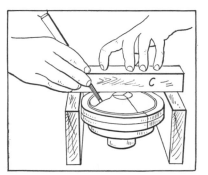

then upon the face surface scribe a circumference equal to the diameter of the hub.

12. Reduce the rim thickness to the dimension represented by *E*, forming a cylindrical projection, as at *K*, of about 3½ inches in diameter. Fig. 232.

Upon the face of the rim thickness, scribe the circumferences represented by *A* and *B*, Fig. 230.

FIG. 233.—Scribing the center lines of the arms upon the raised surface of the web.

Take radii *O* and *P* from templet. Proceed with the aid of templet to turn this face of the pattern to shape.

13. Sandpaper this surface, then scribe circumferences using for the radii *R S* of the templet.

14. Transfer to this face the center lines of the arms, then trace from the paper templet their outline. Figure 233 illustrates, how two blocks are used to support block *C* above the work while scribing the center lines.

15. Turn the convexed surface of the rim. A templet as shown in Fig. 234, is used to test the surface.

16. Dress arms to shape. The arms are roughly shaped by removing the enclosed waste material with a compass-saw as illustrated in Fig. 135, page 126.

FIG. 234.— Templet used in turning the outer surface of the rim.

Following the shaping of the plan view of the arms with a gouge, the narrow blade of a knife is best adapted to rounding the edges of the arms and shaping the beading on the inside of the rim and hub.

THE SURFACE-PLATE AND ITS USEFUL ADJUNCTS

Surface-plate.—A cast iron plate ribbed to give lightness, strength and staying qualities. Machined on all outside surfaces. Used as a base upon which to rest the work when dimensioning or checking distances, or when scribing lines.

Angle-plate.—A cast iron L-shaped bar, machined on faces, edges and ends. Chiefly used as a guide for scriber when scribing lines upon irregular or depressed surfaces.

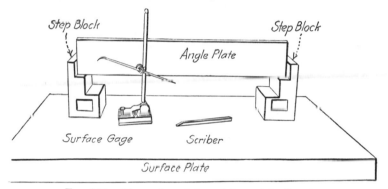

FIG. 235.—The surface plate and its useful adjuncts.

Step-block.—A cast iron step-shaped block machined on all outside surfaces. Used as a guide for scriber and as a support for angle-plate.

Scriber.—A piece of tool steel about $\frac{5}{16}$ inch square and 9 inches long, with one end beveled so as to form an angle of about 20 degrees with one face.

Surface-gage.—A tool with a heavy base supporting a scriber which is adjustable to height. Used chiefly in transferring vertical dimensions from a flat surface to a point on the work.

QUESTIONS

1. What is understood by face-plate turning?

2. Describe a cup-chuck.

3. How is the material prepared for mounting upon a screw-plate or face-plate?

4. What is understood by the center of rotation?

5. Describe and explain the use of the diamond-point and the round-nose tool.

6. Describe the procedure in turning to size the hole in the collar pattern.

7. Why should inside calipers never be used while the work is revolving?

8. What is understood by the term rechucking as applied to turning?

9. What face of a pattern requiring rechucking is usually turned first?

10. For what purpose is the side-tool used?

11. When a piece of work is to be secured to a chuck by friction, how may additional adherence be obtained?

12. How may a circle be scribed upon a revolving surface when the center of rotation of the surface has been destroyed or is inaccessible?

13. Explain the reason for using a templet in shaping the cylinder-head pattern.

14. Why is the depressed surface of the cylinder-head pattern turned first?

15. Describe the method employed in scribing the center lines of the arms of the hand-wheel pattern.

16. What distance is taken and used as the radius when the center of rotation and the surface upon which the circumference is to be scribed are not in the same plane?

17. What is a surface-plate, and for what purpose is it used?

18. What is a surface-gage, and for what purpose is it used?

PATTERN 30

STAR-WASHER

Features presented:
Construction
Half-lap joint
Turning an interrupted surface
Figure 236 is the drawing of a cast iron star-washer.

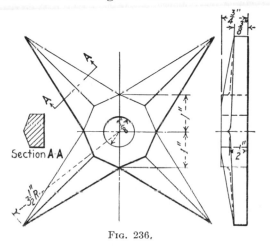

Fig. 236.

If *strength* and *durability* were of no importance, the pattern for the star-washer could be made from one piece of wood. If this arrangement were followed, two of the points of the star would contain *short grain wood and could be easily broken.*

Wood is strongest in a *transverse direction to its grain,* therefore, whenever *durability* is required, the wood should be so *joined together* that its *grain* will lie in such a direction as to give the greatest strength to the pattern.

Two pieces of material *half-lapped together*, as shown in Fig. 237, will make each point of the star lie in the direction of the grain of the wood, and thereby receive its *maximum strength*.

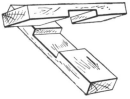

FIG. 237.—The material for the star-washer pattern half-lapped and ready to be glued together.

Stock required: $1 \times 2\frac{1}{2} \times 15\frac{1}{4}$ inches

ORDER OF OPERATIONS

1. Reduce the material to $1\frac{3}{16}$ inch in thickness and $2\frac{1}{4}$ inches in width, then separate it at the middle of its length.

2. At the center of the length of each piece lay out and make a half-lap joint as shown. *Refer to the information on the router, page* 97. *Do not* make the joint so tight that the parts must be forced together, as it will likely *distort* the face of the material.

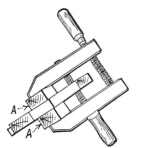

FIG. 238.—The material clamped together while the glue is drying.

3. Glue parts together. Exert the pressure of the hand screws, Fig. 238, *directly* over the glued surfaces by placing blocks *A* between the work and the jaws as shown.

4. Prepare the material. Chamfer the corners *B* as shown in Fig. 239, to *prevent splintering*, and mount the material upon a face-plate.

5. Turn to the greatest required thickness of the pattern. Upon the face scribe arcs of a circumference the diameter of which equals the distance across the points of the pattern. Turn work to this dimension.

Care should always be taken that the tool does not catch in the work when *scribing a line upon or turning an interrupted surface.*

6. Scribe upon the face of the work a circumference which is the diameter of the bolt-hole, and a circumference the diameter of which equals the distance across the corners of the octagon shaped boss.

7. Scribe upon the end surfaces of the material a distance

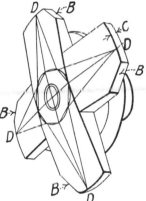

representing the thickness of the points *C*, then turn the face of the pattern to shape.

8. Scribe the center lines *D-D* and lay out the shape of the pat-

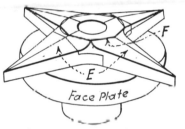

Fig. 239.—The work partially turned and the shape of the pattern laid out upon the material.

Fig. 240.—The face of the pattern in process of shaping.

terns. The work at this stage of completion is illustrated in Fig. 239.

9. Turn the hole to shape and sandpaper the wall.

10. Detach the work from the face-plate and saw the points to shape, then dress their edge surfaces.

11. Lay out the tapered width of the edge surfaces of the points, then re-attach to the face-plate as shown in Fig. 240. By re-attaching the work to the face-plate, the work can be easily secured in the vise.

12. Dress to shape the top surface *E* of the points as shown. Fillets of ⅜-inch radius, as indicated by *F*, connect the surfaces *E* with the outline of the boss.

13. Finish the pattern.

14

PATTERN 31

TOOL-REST

Features presented:
Mounting castings for the operation of machine-finish
The dowel-joint
Shaping pattern
Application of counter-sawing
Figure 241 is the drawing of a cast iron tool-rest. The casting consists of a post supporting a cross-bar.

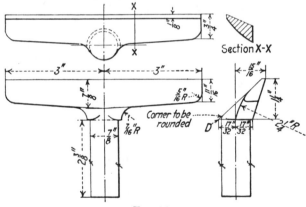

Fig. 241.

Frequently, to facilitate mounting or holding work while performing a machine operation, *a lug or projection* unnecessary in the finished product, nor shown on the drawing, *is to be provided upon the casting.*

Therefore a pattern maker should not only consider the pattern and its mold, but the way the casting is to be *machined.*

Such provision should be indicated on the drawing, but if not so done, *it is no excuse* for its not appearing on the casting, as an efficient workman always feels that his responsibility ceases at the completion of the finished product.

For this reason a pattern maker should be familiar with the various machine shop tools and the methods of mounting work upon them.

The pattern for the tool-rest presents this feature. To turn the surface of the post, the casting is mounted between the centers of the lathe. To *facilitate the drilling* of the hole for the lathe-center into the slanting top surface of the bar, *the lug, H* as shown by the layout, Fig. 242, is provided upon this surface. If an addition of this kind is later found to detract from the appearance of the finished work, *it is removed*.

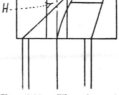

Fig. 242.—The layout of the tool-rest pattern.

A layout of the pattern is required to determine the shape of the joint between the material and the arrangement of the centering-lug. A dowel turned upon the end of the post portion of the pattern affords the means of securing the parts together. The dowel is made to protrude beyond the slanting surface of the bar and thus form the centering-lug *H*.

At the end of the finished surface of the post, a shoulder is formed. The width of the shoulder is $\frac{3}{32}$ inch and represents the amount of finish-allowance removed in finishing the diameter of the post. Ordinarily, $\frac{3}{32}$ inch finish allowance is not enough for the general run of iron castings; however, it will be found sufficient for a casting of this size.

The finishing of the post forms a sharp edge or fin at *D*, Fig. 241. A note specifies that the corner is to be rounded. *This is a machine shop operation.*

Stock required: $1\frac{3}{8} \times 1\frac{5}{8} \times 6\frac{1}{2}$ inch Bar
$1\frac{3}{8} \times 1\frac{3}{8} \times 3\frac{3}{4}$ inch Post

ORDER OF OPERATIONS

1. Turn the post to shape. Make the dowel $\frac{5}{16}$ inch in diameter and $\frac{7}{8}$ inch in length.

2. Dress the material for the bar to the required thickness and length. (Width unimportant.)

3. Scribe the longitudinal and transverse center lines.

4. Bore the hole in the bar material which is to receive the dowel of the post. The position of the hole is more accurately produced if it is bored from *each face of the material to the center of its thickness.*

5. Place post and bar together in their relative positions and trace the circumference of the post upon the surface of the bar.

6. Lay out upon each end of the material the end view of the bar.

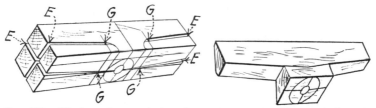

Fig. 243.—Work at the completion of the counter-sawing operation.　　Fig. 244.—The cross-bar in process of shaping.

7. Lay out upon one of the edge surfaces the front view of the bar.

8. Lay out the top view of the bar upon the surface of the material which joins the post.

9. From each end of the material make saw cuts as at *E*, Fig. 243 along the lines representing the top view of the bar and along the lines representing the front view of the bar. The saw cut *stops at the point G* where the fillet which connects the surfaces of the bar with the surface of the post begins. This outline of the bar is *counter-sawed* at this time because the laying out and sawing operation is more easily done while the material is of *rectangular cross-section.*

10. Dress the material to the *triangular* cross-section of the bar as represented by the layout.

11. Complete with the saw the separation of the waste material. The bar at the completion of this operation is shown in Fig. 244.

12. Dress to shape the convex surface of the bar as shown by the cross-section *XX*, Fig. 241.

13. Roughly shape the fillet with a knife, and glue parts together. The pattern at this stage of completion is illustrated in Fig. 245. *The centering-lug is shown at H.*

FIG. 245.—The parts glued together.

14. Complete the shape of the cross-bar. The convex surface of this member is made to gradually disappear into the slanting surface of the bar lying above the post.

The knife is the tool best adapted to the shaping of this surface. In shaping a surface of this nature and which *depends greatly upon the eye;* view the surfaces from different angles as the dressing progresses, to see that they appear the same *each side* of the center line.

MOUNTING THE MATERIAL FOR TURNING PARTED PATTERNS

Features presented:
   Securing together material for parted pattern turning
   Pinch-dogs
   Corrugated fasteners

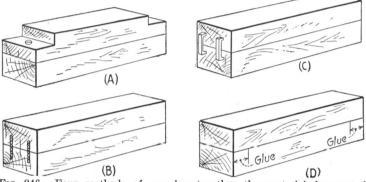

Fɪɢ. 246.—Four methods of securing together the material for parted patterns which are to be turned.

Two pieces of material are secured together and turned as one piece by one of the following methods illustrated in Fig. 246.

Illustration A shows how screws are inserted beyond the limits of the pattern in the waste material. The screws are placed about ¾ inch from the end of the material. About 1¼ inches waste should be allowed at each end of the work for this purpose. If dowel-pins are required, they should be *set* before the material is *secured together*.

Corrugated Fastener.—Corrugated fastener shown in Fig. 247A is a piece of corrugated sheet steel with one edge sharpened. Made in various lengths and widths, the size is designated by the length in inches and the width in the number of corrugations, as ½ inch No. 4, or ¾ No. 7. Corrugated fasteners are used to *secure or reinforce* the joint between two pieces of wood by driving the fastener so that *one half* of its width will be

A

Fɪɢ. 247A.
Corrugated
fastener.

on each side of the joint. The pieces to be secured should be *held in contact* while the fastener is being driven in.

Illustration B shows the application of corrugated fasteners. The fastener should be driven at about the middle of the distance between the axis and the outer surface of the work. When used to temporarily hold two pieces together, as illustrated, the fastener is *not to be driven in flush* with the surface of the wood, but allowed to project $\frac{1}{16}$ inch in order that it may be *withdrawn later* with a pair of pinchers. Fasteners of $\frac{1}{2}$ inch length are best suited for work of this nature.

Pinch-dogs.—Pinch-dogs, as shown in Fig. 247B are used largely when hand-screws will not do. They are used to clamp together adjoining pieces of wood. The inside of the points or legs being tapered, and the outside lying parallel, causes the wood to be drawn together. Their size is designated by the *over-all length* in inches. One inch, $1\frac{1}{2}$ inches and 2 inches, are the sizes chiefly used.

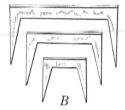

Fig. 247B. Pinch-dogs.

Illustration C shows the application of pinch-dogs.

Frequently it is found convenient to *avoid the use of metal fasteners.* The pieces are then secured together by applying *glue* to the ends of the parting surface of the waste material. as shown in *illustration D.* Sawing off the waste material will release the parts.

When turning small *fragile* patterns, a *strip of paper glued* between the parting surfaces at the center of its length will stiffen and prevent the pieces separating. The pieces are easily separated by the insertion of a knife blade, leaving one half the thickness of the paper adhering to each part.

A mistake frequently made is in not allowing, beyond the limits of the pattern, *sufficient stock for securing the parts together.*

PATTERN 32

LEVER

Features presented:
Mounting castings for the operation of machine-finish
Parted pattern turning
Figure 248 is the drawing of a cast iron clamping-lever.
The casting consists of a handle supporting a boss. The handle
portion of the pattern is turned; the boss is dressed to shape.

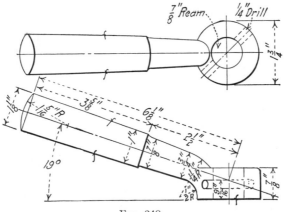

Fɪɢ. 248.

To turn the finished surface of the handle, the casting is
mounted between the lathe-centers. To eliminate the
difficulty of countersinking into the cylindrical surface of the
boss at an *angle*, a hole to receive the lathe-center, a *centering-
lug*, as indicated by *A*, Fig. 249, (*about* $5/16$ *inch in diameter*),
is provided upon the surface of the pattern at this point.
The drawing does not indicate that this provision for
machining the casting is to be made. *Refer to information on*

the mounting of castings for the operation of machine finish; given with Pattern 31, page 210.

Make a side view layout of the pattern as shown in Fig. 250. A layout is required in this case to determine the size of the

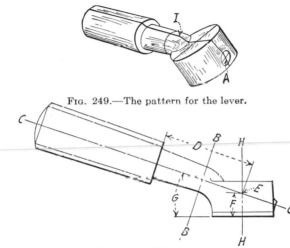

FIG. 249.—The pattern for the lever.

FIG. 250.— The layout of the pattern for the lever.

material; it is also used as a reference from which the dimensions are taken and applied to the turned portion of the handle.

Stock required: $1 \times 2\frac{1}{4} \times 20\frac{1}{2}$ inches.

ORDER OF OPERATIONS

1. Prepare the parting-surface, set the dowels about $\frac{3}{4}$ inch in from the ends of the pattern, then secure the material together with corrugated fasteners. *Corrugated fasteners* afford the cheapest and the quickest means of securing the material together. They are generally used for work of $2\frac{1}{2}$ inches diameter or less.

2. Locate and square around the material the line *B* of the layout, which represents the limit of the turned portion of the pattern.

3. Center the work. This operation requires careful attention; for unless the centers of the lathe are correctly located upon the parting-joint, it will cause an unequal proportioning of the two parts of the pattern.

4. Complete the turned portion of the handle and finish with one coat of shellac.

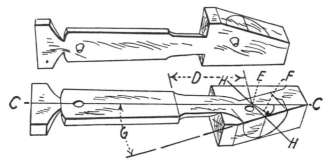

Fig. 251.—The boss of the lever pattern in process of shaping.

Caution: Parted work cannot be turned as close to the axial line as solid work because of the danger of the material breaking off.

5. Separate the work, then upon the parting surface of the drag half locate and scribe the center line C, Fig. 251, of the handle.

6. Lay off upon the center line C the dimension represented by D, obtaining the point E. Using this point as the center and with a radius equal to F, of the layout scribe an arc as shown.

7. Lay out the angle G which the face of the boss forms with the center line C of the handle. The angle is laid out by setting a bevel to the required number of degrees. To scribe this line, place the stock of the bevel along the center line C, and the blade tangent to the arc F.

8. Dress both parts of the material to this angle. The surface produced represents the face of the boss.

9. Scribe the center line H of the boss; then upon the surface which is to be the *face of the boss* scribe a circumference the diameter of which is the diameter of the boss.

10. Make a layout of the boss upon the parting of the drag half of the material. The work at this stage of completion is shown, Fig. 251.

11. Dress the material to this outline of the pattern, then *trace the outline* upon the cope half and repeat the dressing operation.

12. Dress to shape, as at *I*, Fig. 249, that portion of the curved surface of the handle which intersects the top surface of the boss.

13. Scribe the circumference upon the top surface of the boss; then proceed to dress this member to shape.

The fillet connecting the surface of the handle with the surface of the boss and the dressing to shape of the centering-lug is best accomplished with a knife.

PATTERN 33

REDUCING-CONNECTION

Features presented:
  Flange insertion
  Core-print proportioning

Figure 252 is the drawing of a cast iron reducing-connection, consisting of a conical shell supporting a flange at each end.

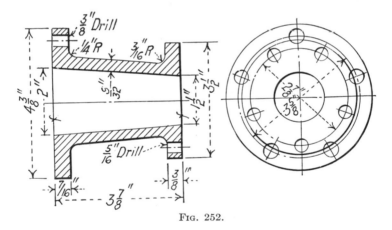

Fig. 252.

The pattern will be parted; core-prints extending out from the ends of the pattern afford the means of supporting the core.

If the grain of the wood in the flanges is laid in the same direction as the grain of the wood in the body of the pattern, the flanges, due to the *short grain,* will be easily broken. This weakness is eliminated by arranging the material as illustrated in Fig. 253.

The flanges are made independent of the body, and with the grain of the wood lying in a transverse direction to the grain of the wood in the pattern body. The flanges are attached by setting them into the body as shown. *Inserting a flange* is the term used to express this method of construction.

The flanges are shown attached to the drag half of the pattern. Attention is called to the way in which the flanges are

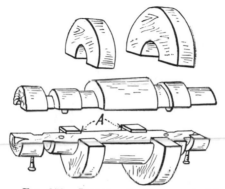

Fig. 253.—Inserting the flange material.

sawed out, permitting their edges, as indicated by *A*, to project above the parting in order that they may later be *planed true to this surface*. The flanges for the cope half of the pattern are shown above the groove into which they are to be inserted and glued.

The diameter of the grooves may be about ¼ inch less than the adjacent diameter of the core-print. The width of the groove is equal to the thickness of the flange of the pattern plus the radius of the fillet.

For the length of the core-prints, *refer to the table of core-print proportions, page 70*. The taper of the core-print is to be the same as the *taper of the shell*.

If the core-prints were made of cylindrical form instead of conical, as shown in Fig. 254, it would not be helpful in the making or in the molding of the pattern, but it would add extra expense in making the core-box. This feature is one that should always be considered, and the core-print portion of a pattern, whenever practicable, should be so *shaped or arranged as to simplify the making of the core-box*.

The layout of the pattern, as shown in Fig. 254, is required in this case to determine the location and size of the grooves for the flanges and the proportioning of the core-prints. It is

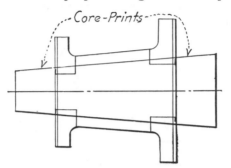

Fig. 254.—The layout of the pattern for the connection.

also used as a reference from which the dimensions are taken and applied to the pattern.

When locating the grooves, make an allowance of $\frac{1}{16}$ inch for turning the outside flange surfaces.

Stock required: $1\frac{1}{2} \times 3 \times 18\frac{1}{4}$ inches Body ⎫
$\frac{7}{8} \times 2\frac{5}{8} \times 9\frac{1}{2}$ inches Flange ⎬ Pattern
$\frac{3}{4} \times 2\frac{1}{8} \times 7\frac{1}{2}$ inches Flange ⎭
$1\frac{1}{2} \times 3\frac{1}{8} \times 6\frac{3}{4}$ inches Core-box ⎫ Core-box
$\frac{3}{4} \times 1\frac{1}{2} \times 6\frac{3}{4}$ inches Core-box ⎭

ORDER OF OPERATIONS

1. Prepare the parting surface and set the dowels.

2. Attach parts together with screws, then center and mount the work. Screws should always be used whenever the work, as in this case, is to be separated before the turning operation has been completed.

3. Turn the material down to the form of a cylinder.

Note: No dimension of the pattern is to be turned to the required size until the flanges are attached.

4. From the center of the length of the material, lay off on each side one half of the over-all length of the body of the pattern; from these lines lay off the width of the grooves.

5. Turn the grooves.

6. Remove work from the lathe and separate the parts.

7. Prepare and saw the flange material to shape, allowing ¼ inch on their diameters for the turning operation. When shaping the concave joint surface, *refer to the information given with Exercise 4, page 26.*

8. Attach the flange material with glue and brads. Drive the brads through the flange from the face adjacent to the coreprint. Set the heads of the brads below the surface, so that they will not come in contact with the turning tool.

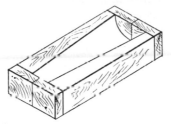

Fig. 255.—The core-box used with the connection pattern.

In preparing the parting surfaces of the *flanges*, make certain that these surfaces are in *contact* throughout their length. This is necessary in order to avoid the *splintering* of the edges of the parting.

9. Remount the work and proceed with the turning operation.

Use the calipers when testing the distance between the outside flange surfaces.

All dimensions are to be transferred from the layout board.

Turn the waste material at the end of the core-prints to about 1 *inch in diameter.*

The core-box for the reducing-connection is illustrated in Fig. 255.

PATTERN 34

RAMMER-HEAD

Features presented:
    Core-print proportioning
    Registering a core
    Application of dowel-pins

Figure 256 is the drawing of a brass butt-head of a floor-rammer.

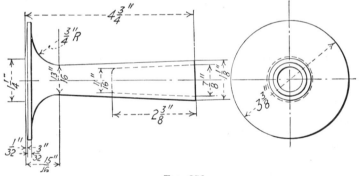

FIG. 256.

The head is secured to a wooden handle by means of a blind socket. The blind socket is formed in the casting by a core placed in the mold as shown in Fig. 257.

When a core receives support from only one end, as in this case, it is sometimes called a *balanced core*.

The core-print must be so arranged and proportioned that the print part of the core will not only *overbalance* that portion of the core which extends into the metal cavity, but it must also prevent the core from rising when pressure is exerted *from below by the inflowing metal*.

Figure 258 illustrates one half of the completed pattern. It will be noted that the diameter of the core-print is made greater than the adjacent diameter of the pattern. Enlarging the diameter of the print in this way has two advantages:

FIG. 257.—Drag part of the mold for rammer-head.

FIG. 258.—The drag half of the rammer-head pattern.

it gives greater *seating surface*, with less length of print, and it provides a *shoulder at A*, which assures the correct registering of the core in the mold.

The pattern in process of making is shown in Fig. 259. The body and the flange material for one half of the pattern

FIG. 259.—Attaching the flange material.

is shown attached. *The neck B*, is the means of attaching the parts together.

A layout of the pattern is required to determine the proportions of the neck, the core-print and the sizes of stock required.

15

Make the core-print about 1⅝ inches in diameter and 1¾ inches long. Make the diameter of the neck ½ inch.

Stock required: 1 × 2 × 18 inches Body ⎱ Pattern
              1⅛ × 2 × 7 ¾ inches Flange ⎰
              1⅜ × 2¾ × 3   inches ⎫
              1⅜ × 1¾ × 3   inches ⎬ Core-box
               ⅝ × 1⅜ × 6   inches ⎭

ORDER OF OPERATIONS

1. Prepare the parting surface and set a dowel at the core-print end of the pattern.

2. Attach parts together *with screws,* then center and mount the work.

3. Turn the material down to the form of a cylinder, then locate and lay off the length of the neck.

4. Turn the neck to size, then rough turn the material to the shape shown in Fig. 259. *Turn no part of the pattern to required size until the flange is attached.*

5. Remove work from the lathe, bore the dowel-pin hole through the neck, then separate the parts. This dowel should not exceed ¼ inch diameter, as a larger dowel would *weaken* the pattern at this point. In order that the dowel may not interfere with the planing operation *the dowel must not be set* until the flange is attached and the parting surface prepared.

6. Prepare and attach the flange material. Allow ⅛ inch on the radius of the flange material for the turning of this surface. *Refer to the information on flange insertion given with Pattern 33,* page 221. Due to the small joint surface obtained between the surface of the neck and the flange, it is important that a *good joint* be made. At the completion of the turning, the joint may be reinforced with brads driven through the neck.

7. Prepare the parting surfaces of the flanges, then set the dowel in the neck, and re-attach parts. A *spot of glue* applied to the parting surfaces of the flange material beyond the limit

of the pattern will help to keep the parts together during the turning operation.

Refer to the information on securing together the material for turning fragile parted patterns, page 214.

8. Turn the face of the flange, then the diameter. Scribe upon the circumference of the flange the edge thickness of this member. Roughly shape the back surface of the flange.

9. Turn to the small diameter of the socket portion of the pattern, then turn the back surface of the flange to shape. A *templet* is used to test this surface.

Fig. 260.—The parts of the core-box shaped and ready to be attached together.

When the diameters of the members of a pattern differ greatly as in the case of the small diameter of the socket portion of the pattern and the flange, the shape of the larger member should be *turned first* as this order of operation tends to *eliminate vibration*.

10. From the face of the flange lay off the over-all length of the pattern and proceed to turn this portion of the pattern to shape.

Figure 260 shows the parts of the core-box for the rammer-head as they will appear when dressed to shape and ready to be assembled.

PATTERN 35

CARBURETOR-CONNECTION

Features presented:
Flange insertion.
Application of templets
Application of the dowel-joint.
Core-box construction
Spoon-gouge

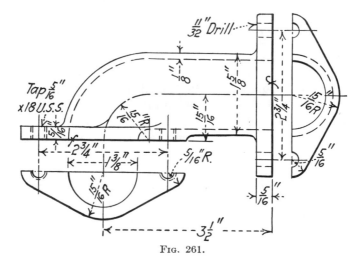

Fig. 261.

Figure 261 is the drawing of a cast iron carburetor-connection, consisting of a shell supporting a flange at each end. The faces of the flanges lie at right angles to each other.

When a view of a casting is the same or symmetrical about a center line, as in the case of the flanges; only a one-half view of the members is sometimes shown.

The pattern is parted. Core-prints extending out from the face of the flanges afford the means of supporting the core.

A layout of the pattern as shown in Fig. 262, is necessary in order to determine the arrangement of the joints between the pattern members.

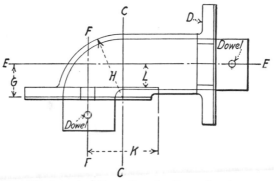

FIG. 262.—The layout of the pattern for the carburetor-connection.

Stock required:

$$\begin{array}{lll} 1 & \times 2\tfrac{1}{4} \times 17 \text{ inches} & \text{Body} \\ \tfrac{5}{8} & \times 2 \ \ \times 8 \text{ inches} & \text{Flange B} \\ \tfrac{1}{2} & \times 1\tfrac{1}{4} \times 7\tfrac{1}{2} \text{ inches} & \text{Flange J} \\ \tfrac{7}{8} & \times 1\tfrac{3}{4} \times 9 \text{ inches} & \text{Core-print M} \\ 1\tfrac{1}{8} & \times 4\tfrac{1}{2} \times 13 \text{ inches} & \\ 1\tfrac{1}{16} & \times 1\tfrac{1}{8} \times 15 \text{ inches} & \end{array}$$

Pattern

Core-box

ORDER OF OPERATIONS

1. Prepare the material for the body of the pattern. For the location of dowels, *see layout.*

2. Locate and scribe around the material the line *C* of the layout.

This line represents the limit of the turned portion of the body.

FIG. 263.—Templet used in tracing upon the material the shape of the flange.

3. Turn the cylindrical portion of the body to approximately 1¾ inches in diameter. Locate and turn the groove which is to receive the flange *D*.

The material for *this flange* is sawed out, attached, and turned in the same way as a flange of circular form.

4. Insert the flange, then remount the work and complete the turning operation. Turn the *diameter* of the flange material to about 3⅝ *inches.*

5. Lay out and cut from thin material or heavy paper, as shown in Fig. 263, a templet corresponding in form to one half of the flange. The radius of the semicircular shape of the templet is equal to the *radius* of the core-print. It is the means of *registering* the templet when transferring its outline to the face of the flange. Dress the flange to shape.

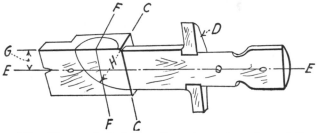

FIG. 264.—The cope half of the pattern at one stage of completion.

6. Locate and scribe upon the parting of the drag half the center lines *E* and *F.*

7. Lay off the distance represented by *G,* and dress both halves of the material to this width.

8. Place the parts together and, using the intersection of the center line *F* with the parting line as a center, scribe upon this surface a circumference, the diameter of which equals the diameter of the shell. From the intersection of this circumference with the parting line, scribe upon the *parting surface the arc H.*

The cope half of the pattern at this stage of completion is shown in Fig. 264.

FIG. 265.—Shaping the surface of the bend with a spoke-shave.

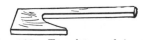

FIG. 266.—Templet used in testing the surface of the bend.

9. Saw and dress the material to the outline of radius *H.*

10. Scribe about the edge surface of the material a distance equal to the semidiameter of the shell, and dress the material to this thickness.

11. Dress the bend to shape. Figure 265 shows this work being done with the spoke-shave. The surface of the material is first dressed to the *shape of an octagon* as shown. Then with the aid of the templet shown in Fig. 266, the dressing of the surface is carried to completion. A block attached to the work affords a means of holding it in a hand-screw.

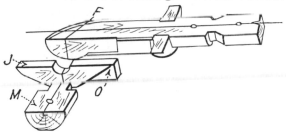

Fig. 267.—The drag half of the pattern at one stage of completion.

12. Prepare the joint surface to receive the flange material *J*, Fig. 267, using the dimensions *K* and *L* of the layout. The drag half of the pattern at this stage of completion is shown in Fig. 267.

13. Fit the material for flange *J* into place, then lay out and dress the flange to the shape shown. Dress to shape the hole through the flange which is to receive the dowel of the core print *M*. Then attach the flange material. The end *O* of the flange is dressed to conform to the cylindrical surface of the shell.

Due to the shape of the core and the position of the two *points of support*, the print *M* is to be made ¾ *inch longer* than the length prescribed by the table of core print proportions.

CORE-BOX FOR CARBURETOR-CONNECTION PATTERN

The dry sand core which forms the interior shape of the carburetor-connection and the box in which one-half of the core is formed is shown in Fig. 268.

The right-hand and left-hand boxes, as they are usually called, are shown in process of making, Fig. 269.

To assure *uniformity* of the two halves of the core-box, the material is doweled together.

Transfer distances C and D from the pattern, then scribe the center lines of the core cavity upon the parting surface and upon the edge and end surfaces of one piece of the material.

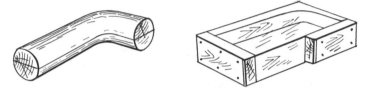

Fig. 268.—The core and one of the core-boxes used in connection with the pattern.

Place the two pieces together and at the intersection of the *center line* and the *parting line* scribe upon one edge and end a circumference, the diameter of which equals the diameter of the core cavity.

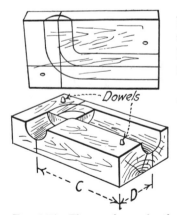

Upon the parting surface of both pieces lay out the shape of the core cavity. *One half* of the box is shown at this stage of completion.

Dress the semicircular portions of the core cavity to the

Fig. 269.—The core-boxes for the carburetor-connection in process of shaping.

Fig. 270.—A spoon-gouge.

required shape. *One half* of the box is shown at this stage of completion.

The surface of the bend is dressed to shape with a *firmer-gouge or a spoon-gouge.* A spoon-gouge is shown in Fig. 270.
Sandpaper the surface of the core cavity, then close the ends as shown.

Plug the dowel holes and finish boxes as instructed.

QUESTIONS

1. What is the object in half-lapping the material for the star-washer pattern?

2. What means may be provided to facilitate the drilling of a hole in a sloping or cylindrical surface of a casting?

3. Why should a pattern maker be familiar with the methods of mounting castings for the operation of machine-finish?

4. What is a dowel-joint?

5. Describe a corrugated fastener and explain its use.

6. How is the size of corrugated fasteners specified?

7. What is a pinch-dog? Explain its action.

8. Explain how glue may be used to secure together material for a parted turned pattern.

9. What feature not shown on the drawing of the lever is to be provided upon the casting?

10. Why should the centering of the material for a parted, turned pattern receive careful attention?

11. What is understood by the term flange insertion?

12. When is the feature termed flange insertion applied to a pattern?

13. What advantage is gained by making the taper of the core-prints of the reducing connection pattern the same as that of the body of the pattern?

14. What is the means used to register the core in the mold for the rammer-head casting?

15. How should a core-print be proportioned for a core lying horizontally in the mold and receiving its support from one end?

16. Why should the flange of the rammer-head pattern be turned before the socket portion?

17. For what purpose is the spoon-gouge used?

PATTERN 36

GLUE-POT

Features presented:
    Application of the suspended core
    Pattern arrangement
    Turning parted work upon a face plate
    Core-box construction

Figure 271 is the drawing of a cast iron glue-pot.

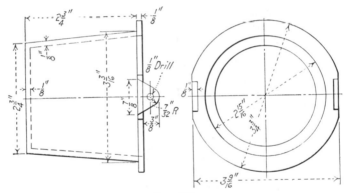

FIG. 271.

FIG. 272.—Sectional view of the mold for the glue-pot.

234

When a casting is of a cross-section similar to that of the glue-pot, the interior of the casting may be formed by a core *suspended* from above the mold as illustrated in Fig. 272. A core-print extending out beyond the flange of the pattern forms a seat at *B*, which registers and supports the core. The contact between the parting surface of the cope and the top surface of the core holds the core in place.

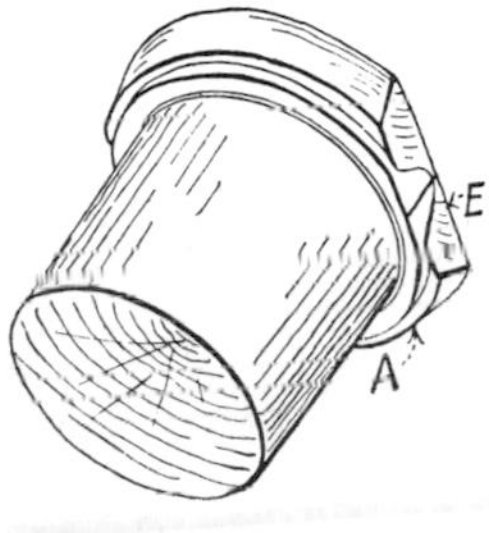

Fig. 273.—The pattern for the glue-pot.

The cavity of the mold which forms one of the ears of the casting is shown at *C*. The impression of the ear is *formed in the core*. The width of the core at *D* is the distance between the outer faces of the ears.

The pattern is illustrated in Fig. 273.

The core-print is made to extend about ¼ inch beyond the flange of the pattern at *A*. The thickness of the core-print is made about ⅝ inch. To assist the setting of the core, a ⅛-inch slant is given the edge of the core-print; this does not apply to the edge surfaces of the core-print at *E*, as only a *slight draft* is given those surfaces.

The grain of the wood which forms the core-print and flange lies in a direction transverse to that of the grain of the wood in the body of the pattern.

Stock required: 3¾ × 3¾ × 3¼ inches ⎱
              1³⁄₁₆ × 4¾ × 4¾ inches ⎰ Pattern
              2¾ × 4 × 12½ inches ⎰ Core-box

CORE-BOX FOR GLUE-POT PATTERN

The core-box in course of making is shown in Fig. 274. One half of the box has been removed from the face-plate and the work carried to completion. The other half of the box shows the material *G* directly above its location in the core cavity. For the purpose of illustration, the ear is shown attached.

ORDER OF OPERATIONS

1. Attach to a face-plate a thickness of facing material. True up the face, then scribe across this surface and in a direction transverse to the grain of the wood, a line passing through the center of rotation.

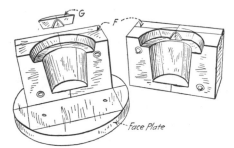

Fig. 274.—Core-box used in connection with the glue-pot pattern.

Whenever securing parted material to a face-plate, *always place the line of parting in a direction transverse to the grain of the wood of the facing material.* Placing the direction of the grain of the wood at right angles gives added strength and eliminates any danger of the facing material *splitting along the line of the parting* of the pattern material.

2. Prepare the material and set the dowels at about the location shown.

3. Select one half of the material and set the edge of the parting surface to the line scribed across the face of the plate. A hand-screw may be used to good advantage for holding the material in place while the screws are being driven. Each half is to be *secured with two screws.*

The parting surface of the material must set perpendicular to the face of the plate in order that the center of rotation may occur *throughout the parting line.*

4. Clamp the two parts together and attach the other half of the material to the face-plate. The material should be further secured by *pinch-dogs.* Drive the dogs into the ends of the material about 1 inch back from the face of the work.

5. True up the face of the material, then scribe a line through the center of rotation and at right angles to the parting line.

6. Locate and scribe, parallel to the parting, the lines F, which represent the position of the outer face of the ears.

7. Scribe upon the face of the material a circumference whose diameter is that of the core-print of the pattern.

8. Turn out the core-print portion of the box to shape. Scribe circumferences upon this depressed surface to represent the diameter at the top and the diameter at the bottom of the interior of the casting.

In turning this portion of the box to shape, it is important, *because of the depth* of the core cavity, that the supporting edge of the tool-rest be set about *parallel* to the surface being turned. As the turning progresses, the tool-rest is moved *farther* into the cavity.

9. Fit the material for the pieces G into place. Make the pieces of ample width so that they may be held in place so that the line F may be transferred to their top surface. The material is then dressed to this line and the pieces attached.

10. Dress the ears to shape. Sandpaper their edge surface before attaching.

PATTERN 37

WATER-JACKET

Features presented:
A matched parting
Mounting work for turning
Core-box construction
Figure 275 is the drawing of a cast iron water-jacket for a glue-pot.

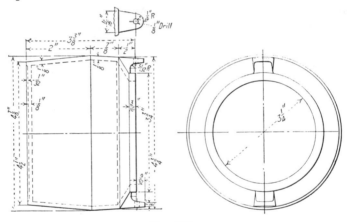

FIG. 275.

The two parts of the pattern are registered by what is commonly called a *matched parting*, as shown in Fig. 276. The illustration shows the pattern in a position reverse to that in which it is molded.

A matched parting consists in forming a projection upon the parting surface of the cope part of the pattern, as at *A*, and a corresponding depression in the parting surface of the drag part of the pattern.

238

The diameter of the projection or dowel may be made about three-quarters of the diameter of the parting surface, and about ¼ inch in length. A slant of about 1⁄16 inch is given the edge surface of the projection.

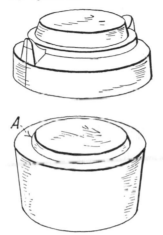

Fig. 276.—The pattern for the water-jacket.

The customary procedure in making a matched parting is to complete one of the parting surfaces, then turn the other parting surface *to fit it*.

Stock required: 2 × 5¼ × 5¼ inches ⎫
3¼ × 5½ × 5½ inches ⎬ Pattern
2 × 3½ × 13½ inches ⎫
2⅜ × 3½ × 13½ inches ⎬ Core-box

ORDER OF OPERATIONS

1. Mount the material for the cope part of the pattern and turn the parting surface. *Do not detach from the face-plate.*

2. Mount upon another face-plate the material for the drag part of the pattern, and turn the parting surface to conform to the parting surface of the cope part.

3. Detach the drag part from the face-plate and secure it to the cope part with a screw inserted through the work at the center of rotation.

4. Turn the material to the greatest diameter of the pattern, then lay off from the parting line distances to represent the thickness of the cope and the drag section.

5. Turn the drag part of the pattern to shape. Allow waste to remain about the screw which secures the parts together.

6. Turn the cope part of the pattern to the required diameter and detach the parts.

7. Rechuck the cope part of the pattern and complete the turning operation.

8. Dress the ears to shape and attach.

CORE-BOX FOR WATER-JACKET PATTERN

The core-box for the water-jacket is shown in Fig. 277. The information on attaching material to a face-plate for

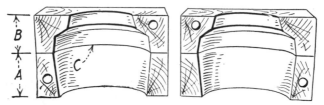

Fig. 277.—Core-box used in connection with the water-jacket pattern.

turning *parted work* given with the core-box for glue-pot also applies to the core-box for the water-jacket pattern.

Two separate turning operations are made in forming the core cavity. Part *A* and *B* are turned independently and glued together along the line at *C*. Dress the material to the required thickness *A* and *B* before attaching it to the face-plate.

PATTERN 38

PISTON

Features presented:
Core-box construction
Fitting small bosses to irregular surfaces
The Fostner-bit

Figure 278 is the drawing of a cast iron piston.

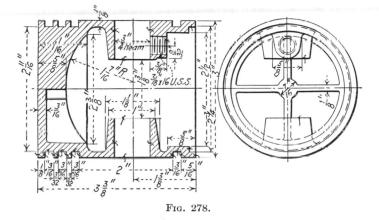

FIG. 278.

The entire exterior surface of the piston casting is required to be finished. No attention will be given the grooves for the rings, this is a machine shop operation. The ¾ inch diameter holes for the wrist-pins are required to be reamed. *Refer to the information on finished holes given with Pattern 11, page 105.* Like the glue-pot casting *Pattern 36, page 234* the interior of the casting is formed by a *suspended core.*

Figure 279 illustrates the pattern.

A core-print of about 4 inches in diameter makes a projection at *A* and in the mold forms a seat which supports the core.   Make the thickness of the core-print about ⅝ inch.   The edge of the core-print is to be given ⅛ inch slant.

FIG. 279.—The pattern for the piston.

Stock required: 3¾ × 3¾ × 4   inches ⎫
                ¾ × 4   × 4   inches ⎬ Pattern
                1⅝ × 5½ × 5½   inches ⎫
                1⅝ × 2⅞ × 11½ inches ⎬ Core-box
                1⅜ × 2⅞ × 11½ inches ⎭

Figure 280 illustrates the core-box.   To better show the interior of the core cavity, a portion of the box has been removed.

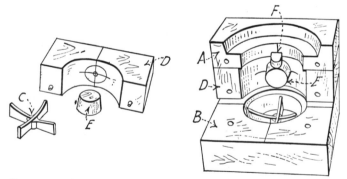

FIG. 280.—Showing the arrangement of the core-box for the piston.

Part A of the box is turned.   The depression in *part B* of the box is turned.   The ribs are made as shown at *C*, and attached in place.   *Part D* is sawed to shape.   Bosses *E* may be turned or sawed, and sanded to shape, and glued to *part D*.   Lug *F* is made and attached to boss *E*.

The Fostner Bit.—The Fostner bit, as shown in Fig. 281, is so designed that it bores a hole with a *flat bottom*. This

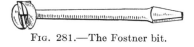

FIG. 281.—The Fostner bit.

feature makes this type of bit well adapted for forming seats for small round bosses in concave or convex surfaces. It is also used to a good advantage in removing the *excess waste* from an inclosed depressed surface that is to be finished with the router.

With a 1⅛-inch Fostner bit, form seats to receive the bosses *E*. This method of attaching bosses of a small diameter to a curved surface, is in most cases preferable to dressing the boss to fit the surface.

Frequently it is advantageous to locate the center of a boss and dress it to shape after the material is in place. In this case, the material is made about ⅛ inch greater in diameter than the required diameter of the boss.

PATTERN 39

HAND-WHEEL

Features presented:
 Loose piece feature
 Application of templets
Figure 282 is the drawing of a cast iron hand-wheel.

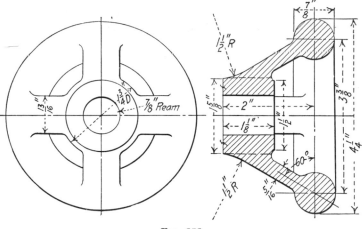

Fig. 282.

Frequently there occurs around the inside of a pattern or a core-box a *ring or projection* which the molding operation requires to be made loose. If the pattern for the hand-wheel were made solid, the rim would not permit the sand which takes the impression of the inside of the pattern to be coped out; *therefore a part of the rim is made a loose piece.*

Figure 283 shows the layout of the work. It is required in determining the position of the joint between the loose piece and the body of the pattern, and in the dimensioning of the pattern.

244

Figure 284 illustrates the mold; the pattern is shown in the sand. In order to remove the loose piece from the body of sand in which it is imbedded, it is parted as at *A*.

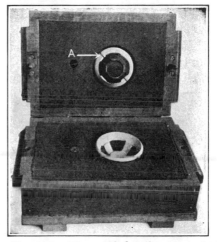

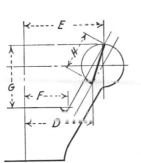

FIG. 283.—The layout of the hand-wheel pattern.

FIG. 284.—The mold for the hand-wheel showing the pattern in the sand.

Stock required: $4\frac{3}{4} \times 4\frac{3}{4} \times 4\frac{1}{2}$ inches Body

$15\frac{}{16} \times 4\frac{1}{4} \times 4\frac{1}{4}$ inches Loose ring

ORDER OF OPERATIONS

1. Prepare and mount the material for the loose piece upon a screw-plate. True up the face, then scribe upon this surface a circumference which is the diameter of the inside of the rim.

2. Turn out a hole of the same dimension, to a depth of $\frac{3}{4}$ inch. Allow stock to remain about the screw at the center.

FIG. 285.—The templet used in testing the inside surface of the rim.

3. Make a templet as shown in Fig. 285 and with its aid turn to shape the convex surface of the rim as indicated by *C*, Fig. 286.

4. Scribe upon the convex surface a circumference whose radius is *D* of the layout. With the aid of a bevel, turn the conical shaped parting surface. Figure 286 shows the loose piece at the completion of this operation.

To give the *maximum strength* to the arms, the grain of the wood must be in the direction of the axis of the pattern.

5. Prepare the material for the body of the pattern and mount it upon a face-plate.

6. Turn to the greatest diameter of the pattern and true up the face of the material. Scribe upon the face a circumference whose radius is *E*, of the layout.

Fig. 286.—The loose ring at the completion of the first turning operation.

Fig. 287.—The body of the pattern at the completion of the first turning operation and ready to receive the loose ring.

7. Turn out a conical shaped depression, the dimensions of which are represented by *EFG*.

8. Scribe upon the bottom surface of the depression the circumference of the hub, then turn this surface of the pattern to shape.

9. Lay off the distance represented by *H* and proceed to turn to shape the parting surface. The *loose piece* is to be used to test the surface as the turning progresses. *Colored chalk* applied to the parting surface of the loose piece will aid the testing operation. The work at this stage of completion is shown in Fig. 287.

10. Secure the loose piece within the body of the pattern by three brads driven from the outer diameter of the work.

Allow the heads of the brads to protrude so they may be withdrawn.

11. Turn the face of the loose piece flush with the face of the body of the pattern. Then with the aid of templet shown in Fig. 285 complete the inside shape of the rim.

templet

Fig. 288 —The exterior form of the pattern in process of turning.

The brads are now withdrawn and brads driven from the inside of the rim, and the exterior form of the pattern turned.

Illustrated in Fig. 288 is the arrangement of the templet used for this operation. The templet is also used to guide the scriber with scribing the center lines *I* of the arms.

12. Space and scribe the center lines *I* of the arms, then lay out their shape.

Remove the waste between the arms by boring a series of $\frac{3}{16}$-inch holes tangent to each other.

Separate the loose piece into two parts with a back-saw.

PATTERN 40

THREE-LEG BASE

Features presented:
Spider construction
Rechucking

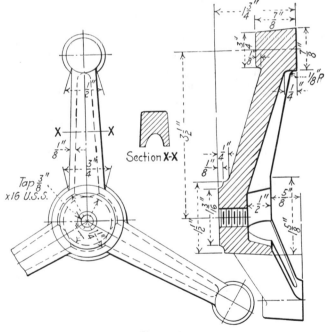

Fig. 289.

Figure 289 is the drawing of a cast iron three-leg base. The casting consists of a hub from which radiate three legs. Pads upon the end of the legs support the casting.

When a number of members of a casting radiate from a center, as in the case of the three-leg base, it is commonly called *a spider*. *Spider construction* is the term commonly applied to this arrangement of material.

When the pattern is comparatively small and the members are of an even number, the material is usually lapped together. If the members are of an odd number, as that of the base, the material is joined together by other means.

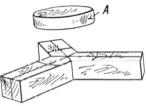

For the base pattern, three pieces of material are joined together as shown in Fig. 290. Glue applied to the *end grain of the wood* cannot be relied upon to hold the material together, therefore the joints are *further secured* by the disc shaped piece *A*, shown above the surface to which it is attached.

FIG. 290.—The material for the base pattern in process of gluing together.

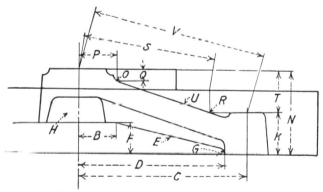

FIG. 291.—The layout of the base pattern.

A partial layout of the pattern, as shown in Fig. 291, is required. It is used as a reference from which location of points and dimensions are taken and applied to the work.

The length of the three pieces of material should be about 5 inches. This length permits the work to be secured to the face-plate for the second turning operation with screws. The screws are inserted through the face-plate and enter the material *beyond the limits of the pattern.*

Stock required: $1\frac{3}{8} \times 1\frac{5}{8} \times 15\frac{1}{2}$ inches
$\frac{3}{4} \times 4 \times 4$ inches

ORDER OF OPERATIONS

1. Prepare (*dress to* $1\frac{1}{4}$ *inch thickness*) and arrange the joints and glue the parts together. Pinch-dogs are best for holding the parts together while the glue is drying. When the glue has set, attach the disc shaped piece **A**.

The depressed surfaces of the pattern are turned first.

2. Mount the work upon a face-plate and true up the face.

3. Scribe a circumference, the radius of which is *B* of the layout. Scribe upon the interrupted surface circumferences whose radii are *C* and *D*.

Caution: Be careful that the tool does not catch when turning or when scribing a line upon an *interrupted surface.*

Keep the tool-rest close up to the surfaces being turned.

Remove the waste material by a *series of light cuts.*

4. Establish the slope of surface *E* by turning a depression whose radius is represented by *B* and depth by *F*, and a semicircular groove of $\frac{1}{8}$ inch radius, as at *G*.

5. Turn interrupted surface *E*, then space and scribe the radial center lines of the legs.

Refer to the instruction pertaining to the scribing of lines upon irregular surfaces, pages 204 and 205.

6. Turn out the depression indicated by *H* and sandpaper its surfaces.

Caution: Do not sandpaper the interrupted surface.

7. Lay out upon the surfaces *E* the outline of the legs, and then dress out the depression as required by the cross-section of the leg, *XX*, Fig. 289.

8. Remove work from the face-plate and scribe the position of the radial center lines upon the ends of the material as at *I* Fig. 292. Scribe upon the edge surfaces of material as at

J, the location of the center line of the pads. Gage lines upon the ends of the material, using the dimension represented by *K* of the layout. The illustration shows the work *rechucked* and ready for the turning operation.

9. To rechuck the work, true up the surface of the facing material, then scribe a circumference, the radius of which is ⅛ inch greater than the radius *D*.

10. Divide the circumference into three equal parts. With glue, attach at these points pieces of about ¼ inch thickness and 3 inches long. The outer edges of the pieces are sawed to conform to the circumference.

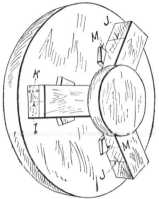

Fig. 292.—The work rechucked.

11. Turn off the face and edge of the strips until they conform to the surface of the legs as at *M*. Each leg of the material is to be secured to the chuck as described.

12. Reduce the material to the dimension represented by *N*.

13. Establish the point *O* by turning a cylinder whose radius is equal to *P* and length to *Q*.

14. Establish the point *R* by turning the interrupted surface, using the dimensions *S* and *T*. A line drawn through these points will represent the slope of the surface *U*.

15. Turn this face of the work to shape.

16. Scribe arcs upon the interrupted surface, using the dimension *V* as a radius.

17. Detach from the chuck, then proceed to transfer to this face of the material the radial center line of the legs.

18. Complete the laying out of the pattern, and dress the work to required shape.

PATTERN 41

TILLER-WHEEL

Features presented:
Construction
Mounting material for turning
Application of a jig
Figure 293 is the drawing of a brass tiller-wheel.

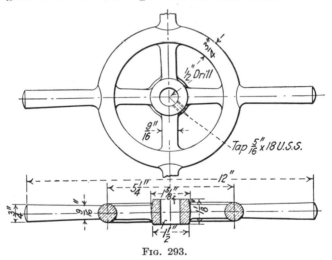

FIG. 293.

Attached to a face-plate, as shown in Fig. 294, is the material.
from which one of the halves of the ring which supports the
spokes is turned. The small area of the cross-section of the
rings makes it advisable to *avoid the use of metal fasteners*.
Therefore, the material is affixed to the face plate by four
strips of paper. The ends of the paper are shown protruding
from the joint at *D*. *Glue* the paper to the face-plate and then
glue the material to the paper.

The insertion of the edge of a chisel at the points of adhesion will cause the paper to split and release the work. To relieve the paper of any *undue strain*, the encircled waste material is secured by *two screws as at E*.

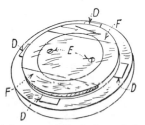

Fig. 294.—The material for one of the halves of the ring mounted upon a face plate.

To give *added strength* to the ring at the points where the semicircular grooves for the spokes are formed in the direction of the grain of the wood, the material is *rabbeted* out and the strips, as at *F*, with the grain of the wood lying in a transverse direction glued in.

Stock required: ½ × 6 ½ × 13½ inches   Rings
             5⁄16 × 1½ × 27   inches   Strips
             1⅜ × 2   × 13½ inches   Spokes
             1 × 1   × 13   inches   Spokes

ORDER OF OPERATIONS

1. Dress the material for the two halves of the supporting ring to rectangular shape, saw the rabbets, and glue strips *F* in place.

2. Dress the material from which the double spoke *A*, Fig. 295, is to be turned, to the required thickness of the hub of the wheel. Dress the material to a parallel width of about 1¾ inches.

3. Scribe the center lines about the material and scribe upon each face a circumference which is the diameter of the hub. Saw the material to the shape shown.

4. Mount and turn the material to the greatest diameter of the spokes. Lay off from the center of the hub the length of the cylindrical portion and the tapered portion of the spokes. Turn the spoke which is toward the *dead-center* to shape and then the spoke which is toward the *live-center*. *This order of turning gives the maximum resistance to vibration.* This member at the completion of the turning will appear as shown at *B*.

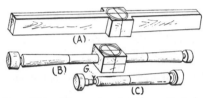

Fig. 295.—The spokes for the pattern in process of shaping.

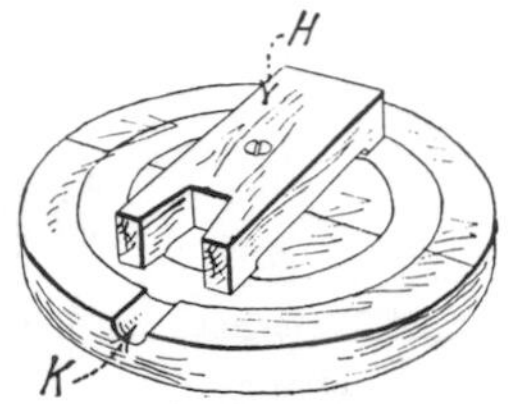

Fig. 296.—Jig used for holding the rings while dressing out the grooves for the spokes.

One of the two other spokes which are turned separately is shown at *C*. The ¼-inch dowel *G* is the means of securing the spokes to the hub.

5. Prepare the material for the two halves of the supporting ring (*dress to required thickness*), and attach to a face-plate as instructed. The use of two face-plates will expedite the work.

6. Scribe upon the face of the material circumferences at the inside and the outside of the ring. Separate the ring from the enclosed waste with a diamond-point or side-tool. Turn the ring to shape. A *templet* is to be used to test the convex surface.

Figure 296 illustrates how a jig is made by turning a groove in the face-plate which receives and holds the rings while dressing out the semicircular grooves for the spokes. The block *H*, which is attached with a screw, acts as a clamp and holds the ring in the groove.

A groove is dressed out as at *K* to conform to the shape of he spoke. It is used as a *guide* in directing the gouge in cutting to shape the grooves in the rings.

To give the *maximum strength* to the construction, the grain of the wood in the two rings should be placed in a *transverse direction*.

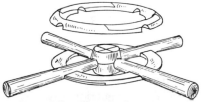

Fig. 297.—The members of the tiller-wheel pattern shaped and ready to be glued together.

Figure 297 shows how the members of the pattern will appear when shaped and ready to be glued together.

Assemble the members, and inspect the joints. *Mark* the position of the parts, that there may be no *delay during the gluing up operation*.

Blocks placed between the hardwood jaws of the handscrews and the rings during the gluing up operation, will prevent the defacement of the surface of the pattern.

PATTERN 42

CHAMBER

Features presented:
    Coring holes in pipe-connection castings
    Joining material of a semicylindrical cross-section
    Application of a jig
    Supporting work upon saw-table
    Combination core-box
Figure 298 is the drawing of a brass chamber.

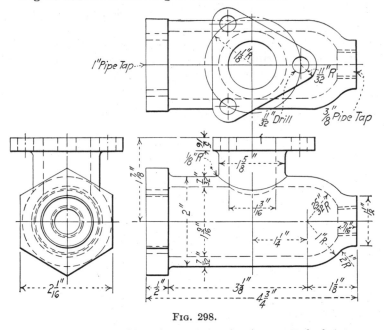

Fig. 298.

The drawing specifies that an opening in one end of the casting is to be tapped to receive a 1-inch diameter pipe. A hole

256

in the other end of the casting is to be tapped to receive a ⅜-inch pipe.

The approximate outside diameter of a 1-inch standard pipe is 1⅚₆ inches (1.31″). The approximate outside diameter of a ⅜-inch standard pipe is $\frac{43}{64}$ inch (.675).

The usual practice (unless otherwise instructed) in the case of cored holes which are to be tapped to receive a pipe, is

Fig. 299.—The parts of the drag half of the pattern ready to be attached together.

to make the *diameter* of the core the *size* of the pipe specified. A cored hole of this dimension will give sufficient finish allowance for the *enlarging and tapping operation*.

Figure 299 illustrates the shape of the joint made between the branch and the body of the pattern. This shape of joint is used when the diameters of the members are equal or approximately equal. When the diameters are equal, the angle of the joint surfaces will be a *right angle* and the junction of the cylindrical surfaces *will miter*.

If there is a slight difference in the diameters, as in the case of the two members of the chamber pattern, the angle of the joint surfaces will be greater than 90 degrees, and the cylindrical surface will not miter. This slight difference will be corrected by the fillet affixed along the line of intersection.

The flange *A* of the branch and the hexagonal wrench-grip portion *B* of the body are to be turned to the dimension across the corners, then laid out and dressed to shape.

Figure 300 shows the shape of the joint between the parts laid out upon the parting of the drag half of the body. The distance *C*, that the branch enters the body of the pattern, is

17

obtained by making a cross-section layout along the center line of the branch.

Note how strips as at *D* are bradded to the ends of the core-prints to cause the parting surface to lie parallel to the

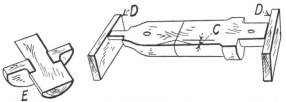

Fig. 300.—Method of supporting the body of the pattern, while the opening which is to receive the branch is being sawed to shape.

table while the outline of the joints is being sawed. The branch as it will appear at the completion of turning is shown at *E*.

CORE-BOX FOR THE CHAMBER PATTERN

The parts which make up the core-box for the chamber casting are shown in Fig. 301.

Fig. 301.—The parts of the core-box shaped and ready to be attached together.

To make a right and a left half-core which are subsequently pasted together, the branch cavity is formed to the *right* and to the *left* of the center line of the box as at *A* and *B*. Above the cavity *A* is shown the *stop-off piece C*. The stop-off piece conforms to the shape of the cavities and is the means of closing them. *One half* of the core is made with the stop-off piece placed in *cavity A*. The other half of the core is made with the stop-off piece placed in *cavity B*. The spherical surface of the core cavity *D* is turned.

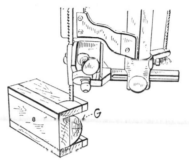

FIG. 302.—Sawing by the aid of a jig the shape of a joint surface.

The information given pertains to the required pattern. When the difference between the diameters of the body of a pattern and of a branch will not permit of the making of the joint by the method described, the joint is then sawed to shape by attaching the branch material, as at *G*, within a jig as shown in Fig. 302.

The outline of the joint surface is scribed upon the top surface of the jig.

PATTERN 43

ELBOW WITH SIDE OUTLET

Features presented:
    Construction
    Loose flange application
    The slab-core
    Locating a core without a print depression
    Application of dowel-pins
    Application of a jig

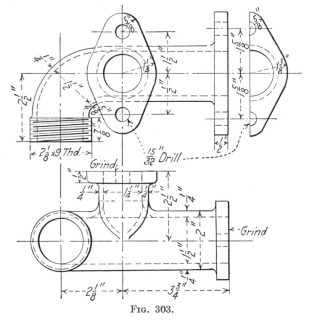

FIG. 303.

Figure 303 is the drawing of a cast iron elbow with side outlet.

A study of the distinctive shapes that go to make up a casting, *a layout* of the pattern, and a *fair knowledge* of what can be done on the machines, reduces the bench-work to the minimum. This feature is illustrated by the pattern for the elbow, as it may be made practically upon the *lathe*, the *band-saw* and the *sander*.

The drag part of the pattern is shown in Fig. 304. The flange *C* is shown directly above the position it occupies upon the part *B*. The flange is made *loose*. When the ramming of

FIG. 304.—The drag part of the elbow pattern.

FIG. 305.—The slab core used in connection with the pattern.

the sand has reached the height of the face of the flange, it is struck off level with this surface. The flange is then drawn out and its depression covered by a *slab-core* as shown in Fig. 305. The slab-core is located and held in place by the hole through the core which engages the core-print of the pattern. The mold is then carried to completion in the usual way.

Make the slab-core about ¾ inch in thickness and 1½ inches greater in width and in length than these dimensions of the flange.

The adjacent parts of the body of the pattern may be secured together with glue and brads or by turning dowels upon part *A* and part *E*, and inserting the dowels into the bend portion *D* of the pattern.

The flange *C* is located upon part *B* by being received upon the neck *G*. The diameter of the neck is equal to the diameter of the core-print *F*. The position of the flange is registered by a *small dowel-pin*.

When the dimension of a surface will not permit the use of a stock dowel-pin, a *heavy brad* may be used. The width of the shoulder upon which the flange rests will not permit of the use of a stock dowel, therefore a *brad* should be used.

Use the brad as a *drill-point*, and bore a hole through the flange into the shoulder. Drive the brad through the flange.

FIG. 306.—The parts of the pattern in process of shaping.

Cut off the brad about ⅛ inch from the surface of the flange with a pair of nippers, then point it slightly with a file.

Figure 306 shows the component parts of the drag half of the pattern. Parts *A* and *E* need no explanation.

Turn part *B* to the required diameters. It should be of ample length, as indicated by the *dotted lines*, to permit of

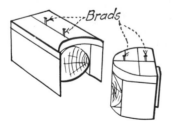

FIG. 307.—The jig used in sawing to shape the joint surface of part *B*.

its being sawed to fit the convex surface of part *A* as shown. The sawing operation is accomplished by securing part *B within a jig as shown in* Fig. 307. An arc which represents the outline of the surface to be sawed, is scribed upon the top surface of the jig, and the combination separated, as shown.

The material for flange *C* is sawed in the form of a *disc*. It is mounted upon a face-plate, and the fillet and the hole at the center turned. Its shape is then laid out and the work sawed and sanded to this outline.

The bend part D is made by turning a ring whose radii are that of the radii of the bend. The ring is then divided into four equal parts, as shown, and two 90-degree segments cut from it. *The grain of the wood* of the two segments to be used is to lie in the direction of their greatest chord.

Verify the shape and the dimensions of the parts by assembling one-half of the pattern *upon the layout.*

Allow glue to set, *then use this half* in the assembling of the opposite half. Reinforce the joints with brads. The brads should be toed.

CORE-BOX FOR THE ELBOW PATTERN

Figure 308 illustrates the core which forms the interior surface of the elbow casting. It is made in two halves; the two halves being pasted together *along the line A*

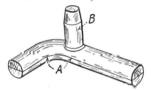

Fig. 308.—The core used in connection with the pattern.

The core-box which forms one-half of the body core and the outlet portion B, is shown in Fig. 309. This half of the core can be made without parting the box as shown. However,

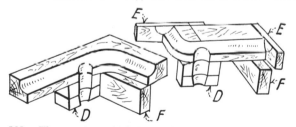

Fig. 309.—The core-box which forms the outlet portion of the core.

this feature facilitates the core work, as it makes possible the removal of the box from the core with the *least disturbance to the sand.*

Figure 310 illustrates the core-box at one stage in its making. The parting has been made (*sawed*) and the outline of the core cavity laid out. The saw cut will cause a variation to occur on the convex surface of the parting, and also upon the edge

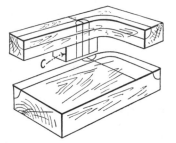

Fɪɢ. 310.—The core-box in process of making.

and upon the end of the material. This is to be corrected and the block *C* attached, before proceeding with the laying out of the cavity.

The core-print portion *D*, Fig. 309, of the box is made independent of the box and then attached. The ends of the core cavity are closed by the pieces *E*. The cleats *F* support the box in a level position.

The instruction given with the core-boxes for pattern 35, *page* 232, also applies to the core-box (not shown) for one-half of the core for the elbow.

PATTERN 44

HOSE-CONNECTION

Features presented:
  An irregular parting surface
  Bedding in a pattern
  Core-print arrangement
Figure 311 is the drawing of a cast iron hose-connection.

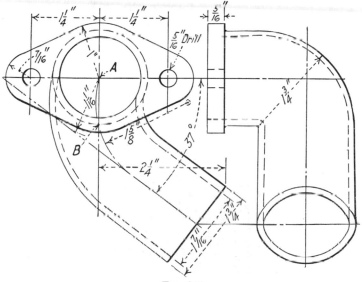

FIG. 311.

The parted patterns heretofore discussed have had a
straight parting surface. An *irregular parting* surface is
presented by the pattern, Fig. 312, for the hose-connection.

The shape of the parting is made to conform to the center
line of the casting with this exception: instead of the parting

surface following the arc of the 1⅝-*inch radius* until it reaches the intersection of the center lines at *A*, Fig. 311, the curved surface of the parting stops at the point *B* where the arc intersects the circumference of the pattern.

Terminating the curved surface of the parting at the point *B*

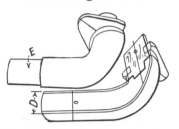

and making the surface from there on straight, simplifies the making of the flanged end of the pattern.

Patterns of this character are usually *bedded in.* This molding operation consists of filling the drag flask with sand and forcing the pattern down to the desired position. The sand

FIG. 312.—The pattern for the hose-connection.

is then firmly tucked and rammed about the pattern and the parting made, as shown in Fig. 313.

An arrow indicates the direction in which the pattern is *drawn from the sand.* In order to do this, the parting is arranged as at *C*, and the impression of the end of the core-print is taken by the *sand of the cope.*

FIG. 313.—The drag part of the mold for the connection showing the pattern in the sand.

Drawing the pattern in this direction requires that the diameter of the core-print of this half of the pattern be made equal to the diameter of the pattern as shown at *D*, Fig. 312.

The core-print of the cope part of the pattern as at E, is dressed to the shape shown. If the cope half of the core-print of the pattern were made to correspond to that of the drag half, it would be necessary to form a shoulder in both halves of the cavity of the core-box. This shoulder would *interfere* with the removal of this half of the box from the core.

Figure 314 illustrates the pattern in course of making. The parting has been arranged, the dowel F set, and the cylindrical portion of the body of the pattern turned.

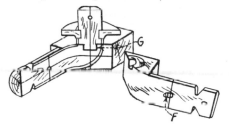

FIG. 314.—The pattern in process of making.

Bore the holes for the dowel pins in the *direction in which the pattern separates with the mold.*

To turn, secure the parted end of the material together in the usual way. Secure the parting surfaces together beyond the bend with pinch-dogs.

A dowel-joint is used as at G, to secure the flange portion of the pattern to the body.

Trace from a paper templet the outline of the bend upon the parting surface.

On account of the position of the core in the mold and its points of support, the core-print at the *flanged end* of the pattern is to be made ¾ inch greater in length than that prescribed by the table of core-print proportions.

CORE-BOX FOR THE HOSE-CONNECTION PATTERN

There would be no advantage in the forming or in the drying of the core for the hose-connection if it were made in halves, then pasted together. Therefore the box is made as shown in course of construction, Fig. 315. The parting has been arranged and the outline of the core cavity laid out.

The arrows indicate the direction the box separates. The dowel-pins are set accordingly.

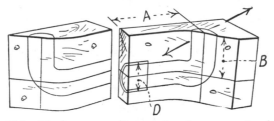

FIG. 315.—The hose-connection core-box in process of making.

Verify the shape of the parting of the core-box with the parting surface of the pattern.

Transfer from the pattern the distances *A* and *B*. Transfer to this surface of the core-box, by the aid of a paper templet, the outline of the core made upon the *parting surface of the bend of the pattern.*

The enlargement at the end of one-half of the core cavity at *D* is made to correspond to the core-print portion *D* of the drag half of the pattern, Fig. 312.

PATTERN 45

RING

Features presented:
Segmental construction
Figure 316 is the drawing of a cast iron ring.

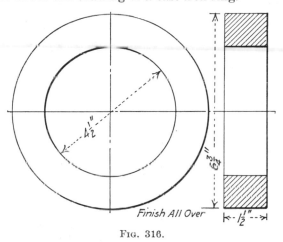

Finish All Over

Fig. 316.

Ring patterns made of one piece of wood cannot be *relied upon to retain their form;* therefore they are built up by what is termed *segmental construction.*

Segmental construction consists in laying upon one another a series of rings or courses, each course consisting of a number of parts called *segments.*

The grain of the wood in the segments lies in the direction of the greatest chord of the segment, and thereby gives the maximum length grain wood around each course. The *strength* of a pattern built up by this construction is proportional to the *number of courses* and the *number of segments* to a course.

269

Courses for patterns up to 14 inches in diameter may consist of four segments, but from 14 to 36 inches in diameter it is the common practice to use six.

The accompanying table of chords dividing a circle into from 3 to 24 equal parts will be found very useful when applied to segmental and stave construction.

The quantities in the columns headed *A* are the number of segments or staves required to a circle.

To obtain the length of a chord, multiply the diameter of the circle upon which the chord is to be laid off by the quantity found in columns *B* opposite the number of segments required.

TABLE OF CHORDS

A	B	A	B	A	B	A	B
		7	.4338	13	.2393	19	.1646
		8	.3826	14	.2225	20	.1564
3	.8660	9	.3420	15	.2079	21	.1490
4	.7071	10	.3090	16	.1950	22	.1423
5	.5877	11	.2817	17	.1837	23	.1361
6	.5000	12	.2588	18	.1736	24	.1305

It is often more convenient to lay segments upon a faceplate, then face the joint in the lathe. However, this procedure is not necessary, as the joints between courses may be *planed*. Add about $\frac{1}{16}$ inch to the *thickness* of segments when the joint between courses is to be turned.

Whenever the cross section of a member will permit, it is a good practice not to depend entirely upon the glue, but to nail the segments as well. *Nailing hastens the work*, as it eliminates clamps and the delay of waiting for the glue to dry.

To obtain the maximum strength, the joints between the ends of the segments are placed midway between those of the preceding course.

Build up the work perpendicular to the surface upon which it is laid.

Do not fit a course of segments together and then proceed to lay them, *but rather fit and glue each segment in sequence.*

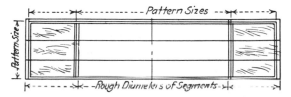

Fig. 317.—The layout of the ring pattern.

Make a layout of the cross-section of the pattern as shown in Fig. 317, then scribe lines to represent the thickness and the width of the segments. The thickness of the courses is to be *equally proportioned.* The ring pattern will be built up of three courses. The courses will be made up of four segments. It would be a waste of time to lay out the shape of each segment, therefore one segment is laid out and sawed to shape. It is used as a *templet* to trace the outline of the other segments upon the material as shown in Fig. 318.

 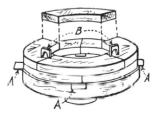

Fig. 318.—Outline of segments traced upon the material.

Fig. 319.—The pattern for the ring in process of building.

Allow for the turning operation $\frac{1}{4}$ inch of waste material upon the inside and the outside edges of the segments. Upon the ends of the segments allow $\frac{1}{16}$ inch for fitting them together.

Figure 319 shows the laying of segments upon a face-plate.

The segment which completes the second course is shown directly above the surfaces to which it is glued.

To prevent the segments being affixed to the wood-facing of the face-plate by the glue forced out of the joints, *strips of paper*, as at *A*, are glued to the facing at these points.

ORDER OF OPERATIONS

1. Scribe a circumference which is the outside diameter of the layout of the work. Dress both ends of a segment (*use trimmer or sander*) then set its outer edge to coincide with the circumference scribed. Secure the segment to the plate with two brads.

2. Dress both ends of the next segment, then fit it in place. Apply glue to the abutting ends and drive in a pinch-dog as at *B*. Secure this segment to the plate with brads. Proceed in a like manner to attach the next segment.

3. Place the last segment of the course above its location and transfer to its under surface with a scriber the length of the opening it is to fill. Dress the segment to this length and secure it in place. Set the brad heads.

4. True up the face of the segments, then proceed to lay and glue on the next course. *Verify the height* of each course with the layout.

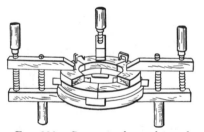

FIG. 320.—Segments clamped together with hand-screws while the glue is drying.

5. Turn the pattern to size and finish in the usual way.

To detach the pattern, insert edge of chisel between plate and work, and carefully pry apart.

If the brads are found to remain in the work, they may be pulled out with pinchers, or cut off with a pair of nippers and driven back with a nail-set.

When the cross-section of a member will not permit the use of brads, hand-screws are used, as shown in Fig. 320, to clamp the segments together while the glue is setting. The glue will take about 30 minutes to set.

PATTERN 46

HOUSING

Features presented:
Three part mold
Application of templet
Segmental construction
Figure 321 is the drawing of a cast iron housing.

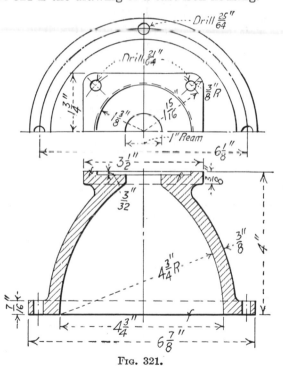

FIG. 321.

If segments of the *same radius* were used in building up some patterns, it would cause an *excessive waste of material*.

The selection of the housing pattern is to present a method which makes possible the *saving* of this material.

When a pattern is built up of courses of varying diameter, as in this case, the course of segments of the greatest diameter *is laid first.* This order of procedure gives a better support

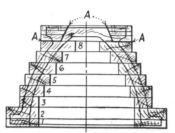

to the work and facilitates the clamping together of the segments. Due to the shape and the *cross-section* of the shell, *brads are not to be used.*

The layout required of the pattern is shown in Fig. 322. It shows the number of courses and how the diameter of the course *varies with the section* of the pattern. The square flange

FIG. 322.—The layout of the housing pattern showing the arrangement of the segments.

is made loose; the parting line is indicated by *A*.

Verify with the layout the *distance* at which the joint between each course of segments occurs above the surface of the face-plate. A disc equal in diameter to the last course of segments closes the top and completes the building-up operation.

Loose-flange. Build up the *loose flange* of *three courses of segments.* Make the diameter of the courses about ½ inch greater than the distance across the corners of the flange. Turn the parting surface and the thickness of the flange, then dress the flange to rectangular shape.

Turning the body of the pattern. True up the face of the work, then detach it and *remount it in the reverse position.* Turn the face of the flange.

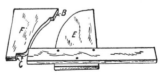

FIG. 323.—Templets used in testing the surface of the pattern.

The joint between courses *one* and *two* should occur at about the center of the thickness of the flange.

Turn the interior surface. The circumference of the inside diameter of the pattern scribed upon the face of the flange *locates* the position of the templet *E* shown in Fig. 323. The cross-bar of the tool-rest is to *project* into the work so that it will give support to the tool near the cutting-edge.

Rechuck the work and turn the flange to the required diameter and thickness. Turn the work to the over-all height of the pattern. Turn the parting surface A to fit the parting surface of the loose flange.

Turn the exterior shape of the pattern. The templet *F*, shown in Fig. 323, is used to test this surface. The templet is located by the surface *B* being brought into contact with the parting surface which receives the loose flange and the surface *C* of the templet into contact with the corner of the flange of the body of the pattern.

Molding the Pattern.—A *three-part mold* is used to take the impression of the housing pattern. As the name implies, a three-part mold is made up of three sections, namely, a *cope*, a

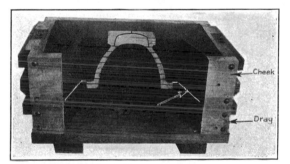

Fig. 324.—Sectional view of the drag and check parts of the housing mold showing the pattern in the sand.

drag and a section which lies between the cope and the drag, called a *cheek*. A cross-section of the mold as illustrated in Fig. 324, shows the pattern imbedded in the sand of the cheek and the drag. The parting between the cheek and the drag is shown at *D*.

To mold the pattern, ram up a *false cheek*. This preliminary work is done to facilitate the subsequent ramming up of the permanent cheek. Place the *loose flange end of the pattern* upon the mold-board and ram up the false cheek, and make a temporary parting upon which to ram up the drag.

Ram up the drag. Roll the work over, remove the false cheek and shake out the sand.

The parting which is to *separate* the permanent cheek and the drag is now arranged around the edge of the back of the flange as at *D* and the cheek placed in position and rammed up.

Make the parting for the cope, then ram up this section of the mold.

To remove the pattern, lift off the cope, lightly rap the pattern, and draw the loose flange.

The cheek is now lifted off, and the pattern lifted from the sand. The housing pattern may also be molded in a two part flask by using a slab-core. In molding the pattern by this method the large diameter of the pattern is placed upon the mold-board and the drag section of the flask rammed up to the height of the face of the loose flange. A flat surface is struck off at this point and the flange taken out of the sand and its impression covered with a slab-core. The ramming of the drag is then carried to completion and the work rolled over in the usual way. Special arrangement must be made when ramming up the cope for lifting out of the sand from the interior of the pattern.

PATTERN 47

FLYWHEEL

Features presented:
  Three-part lap
  Wheel construction
  Mounting material for turning
Figure 325 is the drawing of a cast iron flywheel.

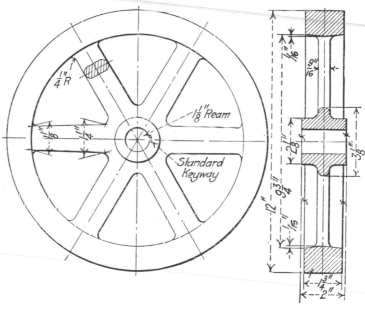

Fig. 325.

The rim of wheel patterns of this type is built up of segmental construction. During the laying of the segments, the arms which have been *partially shaped, are built in place.*

This manner of securing the arms gives the maximum strength to the pattern.

The hubs are turned separately and located upon the spider with dowel-pins. The hub on the cope side of the pattern is parted from the spider. This feature permits the hub to lift off with the cope. The hub on the drag side of the pattern is attached with screws. This manner of attaching the drag hub permits of its detached.

Make a cross-section layout of the pattern as shown in Fig. 326. It is used in determining the thickness and the

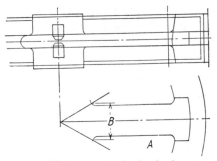

Fig. 326.—The layout of the flywheel pattern.

width of the segment. The dimensions of the pattern are transferred from the layout to the work. Make a layout of one of the arms, as shown at *A*. It is used to obtain the width of the material required for the arms. The width of the material is to be made about ½ inch greater than the distance indicated by *B*.

Allow $\frac{1}{16}$ inch in the *thickness* of the material for dressing the spider to the required thickness.

ORDER OF OPERATIONS

1. Make a three-part lap as shown in Fig. 327, and glue the material for the arms together, then dress to required thickness.

2. Lay out the shape of the arms and saw the spider to shape. Allow about ¾ inch thickness of segments beyond the ends of the arms of the spider.

3. Lay the first course of segments. *Refer to the information on segmental construction given with Pattern 45, page 272.*

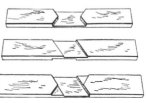

4. True up the face of the first course of segments and lay the second course. *This course of segments is not to be glued.* The segments are to be attached *temporarily with brads* located at *C* Fig. 328.

FIG. 327.—The method of lapping together the material for the spider of the fly-wheel pattern.

5. Scribe upon the face of this course of segments a circumference equal in diameter to the diameter of the spider. Locate the spider upon the face of the segments. The center lines of the arms are to *locate about at the joint* between the ends of the segments. Trace the outline of the ends of the arms upon the surface of the segments.

6. *Detach one of the segments,* saw the openings as at *D* in the ends, and return it to place and *attach it with glue and brads.*

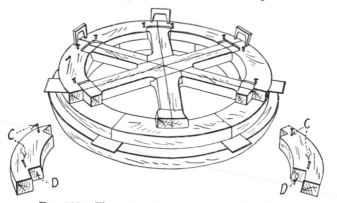

FIG. 328.—The pattern in process of construction.

Removing, then sawing and attaching *one segment at a time* assures the return of the segments to their former position. This operation in process is illustrated in Fig. 328.

7. Turn off the face of the second course of segments *flush* with the surface of the spider and then proceed to lay the next course.

8. True up the face of the work, then turn to the required outside diameter of the pattern.   On each side of the *center of the thickness* of the middle course of segments lay off one half the width of the face of the pattern, and scribe lines which represent this dimension.

9. Turn this side of the pattern and detach from the face-plate.

10. Secure three segments about ¼ inch thick and 3 inches long, to the face-plate with glue and brads, and turn their outer edge to receive the inside diameter of the rim of the pattern.

Attach the work to the face-plate with screws, and proceed to turn this side of the pattern.

The surface of the inside of the rim which lies between the arms and therefore cannot be turned, is dressed to shape.

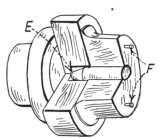

FIG. 329.—Method of mounting the material for the turning of the hubs.

11. Turn hubs to shape.   Figure 329 illustrates the method of centering and attaching the material for the hubs to a face-plate.   A hole is turned in the facing of the plate as at *E*, to receive the dowel set in the hub material.   Dress the material to the required thickness of the hub and attach with brads located at *F*.

12. Place the hubs in position and trace the outline upon the surface of the spider, then round the edges of the arms to conform to the required cross-section.

QUESTIONS

1. What is understood by a suspended core?

2. What should be carefully noted, in regards to the axes of the work, when locating parted material upon a face-plate?

3. What feature should be noted whenever attaching parted material to the facing material of a face plate?

4. What is understood by a matched parting?

5. What is the distinct feature of the Fostner bit?

6. For what purpose is the Fostner bit particularly adapted?

7. What is understood by the term spider construction?

8. When it is desired to avoid metal fasteners, how may the material for small work be attached to the face-plate?

9. What is understood by a jig as applied to pattern work?

10. What is the general practice applied to the diameter of a cored hole that is to be tapped to receive a pipe?

11. What is understood by the term slab-core?

12. What is learned from the elbow pattern?

13. What is understood by segmental construction?

14. What direction should the grain of the wood bear to the direction of the chord of the segment?

15. Where should the joints between the ends of the segments locate in regard to the courses?

16. Upon what feature does the strength of segmental construction depend?

17. Describe the laying of the first course of a ring of segments.

18. What is a three-part mold? Give the name of the parts.

19. What is the object of making a false cheek?

20. What is understood by a three-part lap as applied to spider construction?

21. How should the hubs of wheel patterns be attached to the spider?

22. Why is the layout of a wheel pattern necessary?

23. Describe the method of letting the spider into the segments.

24. Describe a method of attaching to a face-plate small hubs subsequently to the setting of the center dowel.

STAVE CONSTRUCTION

When long cylindrical or conical shaped patterns exceed 8 or 10 inches in diameter, they are usually *built up by stave construction*.

This feature not only gives a light, strong pattern, but it gives one more likely to *retain its accuracy of form and dimension* than if made solid.

The most common practice is to join the staves and attach them to heads as shown in Fig. 330.

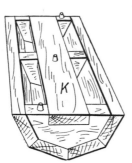

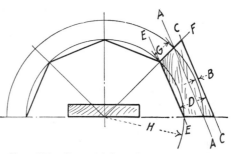

FIG. 330.—Application of stave construction.　　FIG. 331.—Determining the cross-section of staves.

To strengthen the construction and to provide means for rapping and drawing the pattern, the bar *K* is let into the heads as shown.

The heads may be placed about 24 inches apart.

The number of staves will depend somewhat upon the diameter of the work. The thickness of the stave material will depend upon the *strength required*.

If the cross section of the work is made up of a polygon of many sides, the thickness of the staves may be decreased, for less waste will be turned from the corners.

282

For the ordinary run of work, material of 1 inch in thickness will be found suitable for staves.

To determine the number of staves to be used, scribe a semicircumference which is the semidiameter of the cylinder, Fig. 331.

Divide the semicircumference into a number of equal parts and scribe the line *A-A*, which represents the greatest chord of one of the parts.

Lay off the distance *B*, which is the amount of waste to be turned off at this point, then scribe parallel to *A-A* the line *C-C*, representing the outer face of the stave.

From the line *C-C* lay off the distance *D*, which represents the thickness of the stave material, then scribe the line *E-E* and the radial line *F*.

The area enclosed by the lines represents the *cross-section* of the stave.

If the abutting edges *G* of the stave are too thin, divide the semicircumference into a greater number of divisions and repeat the laying-out operation.

The shape of the heads is laid out upon the circumference of the radius *H*.

The thickness of heads should be about one and one half times the thickness of the stave. Lay out one head and accurately saw it to shape. It is then used as a templet in tracing the outline of the other upon the material. The heads are glued and nailed to the bar *K*, then the dowels are set and the staves attached.

By tilting the saw table to the required *bevel* of the edge of the staves, the staves may be ripped to exact shape, thereby requiring no further work to fit them together.

Any slight distortion that is likely to occur through the sawing operation can usually be overcome by the use of pinch-dogs.

If it is desired to make the heads of circular form instead of polygonal, the face of the staves is made concave. The concave surface is formed by passing the staves over a circular-saw at an angle as shown in Fig. 332.

The saw is made to project above the table a distance *equal to the depth of the concavity* to be cut out of the stave. The gage *L* is set and clamped at such an angle that the saw will cut to the width of the *narrow face* of the stave.

To obtain the *angle*, the gage is set to the axis of the saw. Raise the saw to the required distance above the surface of

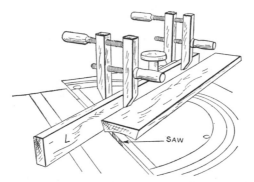

FIG. 332.—Concaving the face of staves upon the saw bench.

the table. Brad together two strips of about 15 inches in length. The *distance* between the inside edges of the strips is to be made *equal* to the narrow face of the stave.

Place the frame over the saw and swing it around until one of the edges comes in contact with the *point* of a tooth at the back of the saw and the other edge comes in contact with a tooth *point* at the front of the saw. Hold the frame in this position and trace the outline of its enclosed width upon the surface of the saw table.

Set the gage *L*, as shown, in front of the saw and to this angle.

To accommodate the bevel on the edge of the staves, the gage is set back from the line traced upon the surface of the table.

A smoother surface will be produced if the waste is removed by two operations. Allow about $\frac{1}{32}$ inch for the finishing cut. *The saw should be sharp and well set, and the staves fed over the saw very slowly.*

Blocks attached to the ends of the work afford the means of securing the halves together and of mounting the work between the centers of the lathe.

Staved Core-boxes. The same principle is involved in the construction of a staved-up core-box, as illustrated in Fig. 333, as that of a staved-up pattern, *only in reverse.*

In the case of a core-box, the inside faces of the staves are dressed to shape, and the outside faces attached to the

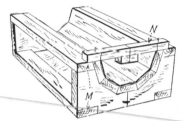

Fig. 333.—Application of stave construction.

heads as shown. Bars connecting the heads, as indicated by M, strengthen the works.

The heads for a staved core-box are laid out in the same manner as for a pattern, except that instead of working from the diameter of the pattern, the number of staves and their cross-sections is found from the *diameter of the core cavity.*

The heads are attached together by the bars M, then the staves glued and nailed in place.

Core-boxes, built up as shown in the illustration, are dressed out to shape with a core-box plane, or with a sole or round-face plane.

Sole Plane. A *sole-plane* is made by attaching wood soles of different face radii with screws to the bottom of a jack-plane. Each sole has a bit of a corresponding radius.

The strip across the top of the box at N is the means of supporting the point of the dividers while scribing the semi-circumference of the core cavity upon the ends of the box.

The semicircular shape of the core cavity can also be produced by passing the staves over the circular saw in the same manner as the staves for a cylindrical pattern were passed.

INDEX

A

Acid oxalic, 47
Adherence, 195
Age of lumber, 2
Air-dried lumber, 2
Alcohol, 46
Allowance, 279
  finish, 54, 211
    aluminum, 54, 93
    brass, 83
    for cast iron, 54
    steel, 54
  for clearance, 97
  for contraction, 42
  for draft, 38
  for dressing to circumference,
    185, 271
    length, 10
    thickness, 10, 278
    width, 10
  for finishing cut, 284
  for fitting, 271
  for paring, 26
  for saw cuts, 148
Aluminum, contraction allowance,
  42
American screw gage, 31
Angle, miter-joint, 154
  parting tool, 172
  plane-bit, 5
  side tool, 195
  stave construction, 284
  to lay off, 69
  with grain of wood, 18
Angle-plate, 205
Arc, center of, 24
  to saw, 26, 126

Arm, hand-wheel, 204
Assembling, 96
Auger-bit, 52

B

Back saw, 30
Balanced core, 120, 224
Band-saw, 15, 26
Barrel, 141
Base, 185
  three leg, 248
Bedding in, 158, 266
Beeswax, 65
Bell-crank, 115
Bench, saw, 99
Bench-hook, 29
Bench-plane, 4
Bench-stop, 11
Bench work, 1
Bent shank, 27
Between centers turning, 160, 216
Bevel, 69
  protractor, 69
Bit, auger, 52
  Fostner, 242
  plane, 4
  twist, 34
Bit-brace, 33
Bit-file, 52
Board-foot, 3
Bolt-hole, 50
Boring, 32, 51, 73, 212
Boss, 79, 83
Bottom-board, 39
Box, core-, 68
Brace, bit, 33
Bracket, 89, 132, 149, 157

287